A Beggar in Purple

By the same Author

HUGH WALPOLE
a biography
THE ARMS OF TIME
a memoir

Edited by Rupert Hart-Davis

THE LETTERS OF OSCAR WILDE
THE LYTTELTON HART-DAVIS LETTERS
and works by
Max Beerbohm, George Moore,
William Plomer, Arthur Ransome, Siegfried Sassoon

A Beggar in Purple

A selection from
the commonplace book of

RUPERT HART-DAVIS

'He wrapped himself in quotations — as a beggar
would enfold himself in the purple of Emperors.'
Kipling

HAMISH HAMILTON
London

First published in Great Britain 1983
by Hamish Hamilton Ltd
Garden House 57-59 Long Acre London WC2E 9JZ

Copyright © 1983 by Rupert Hart-Davis

British Library Cataloguing in Publication Data

Hart-Davis, Rupert
  A beggar in purple: selections from the
  commonplace book of Rupert Hart-Davis.
  1. Quotations, English
  I. Title
  080   PN6081
  ISBN 0-241-11009-2

Filmset by Pioneer
Printed in Great Britain by
Redwood Burn Ltd, Trowbridge, Wiltshire

To my beloved
JUNE
the angel in the house

Contents

Introduction

I have always thought that commonplace book is a misnomer for a pudding full of plums, but the phrase is hallowed by antiquity. In 1642 Thomas Fuller wrote: 'A Common-place-book contains many notions in garrison, whence the owner may draw out an army into the field', and while I was considering how best to set out my forces in battle-array, so that they might resemble a well-drilled battalion rather than an armed mob, I consulted Johnson's great Dictionary, which defines a commonplace book as 'a book in which things to be remembered are ranged under general heads'.

So be it, but some items are not susceptible to such regimentation, and can appear only as a ragged collection of camp-followers, vivandières and miscellaneous other ranks.

For more than fifty years I have copied out poems, sentences, and short pieces of prose which interested, moved or amused me. Most of the poems are now so familiar and often-anthologised that I have sadly rejected them. Some of my special favourites I employed to brighten my letters to George Lyttelton, which have since been published, and it seems unkind to inflict them twice on my few but delightfully persistent readers, so I have retained only a few of them.

I thought of trying to write this brief introduction entirely in quotations, beginning: 'Having grown sluggish and contemplative' (W. B. Yeats) in 'those natural indulgences of old age, anecdote and autobiography' (John Bailey), but I soon decided that I should have difficulty in staying the course. So I simply despatch my troops to battle against oblivion in the hope that they will delight others as they have sustained me.

RUPERT HART-DAVIS

Marske-in-Swaledale
1983

Brevity and Wit

Et les plus sombres d'entre nous
Ont eu leur aube éblouissante.

Victor Hugo

The primary object of a student of literature is to be delighted.

Lord David Cecil

Other people's lives may easily be human documents.
But a man's own life is always a melodrama.

Chesterton

Oscar Wilde, to Ada Leverson:

'My dear Sphinx, I walk about all day with a beautiful young man with a knife in his hand.'

Ada Leverson:

'My dear Oscar, I'm sure he has a fork in his other hand.'

La bêtise consiste à vouloir conclure.

Flaubert

[1]

The past is always attractive because it is drained of fear.

Carlyle

Our lives are in the power of chance.

Gibbon

La Vérité consiste dans les nuances.

Renan

God in the whizzing of a pleasant wind
Shall march upon the tops of mulberry trees.

George Peele

No man can edit the *Leeds Mercury* for thirty years with impunity.

John Morley

'Of this *spilt water* there is little to be gathered up: it is a desperate debt.'

Ben Jonson

C'est une étrange entreprise que celle de faire rire les honnêtes gens.

Molière

Cette vie est un hôpital où chaque malade est possédé du désir de changer de lit.

Baudelaire

O, what a world of vile, ill-favour'd faults
Looks handsome in three hundred pounds a year.

Shakespeare

It looks well in the newspapers, and almost anything that does that is horrible.

Henry James

When Lord Lonsdale presented the Hawthornden Prize to Siegfried Sassoon [in fact S. S. wasn't there], Augustine Birrell said 'How refreshing it is to hear a speech made by somebody who can't'.

Would that he [the whale] consumed his own smoke! For his smoke is horrible to inhale, and inhale it you must, and not only that, but you must live in it for the time. It has an unspeakable, wild, Hindoo odour about it, such as may lurk in the vicinity of funereal pyres. It smells like the left wing of the day of judgment; it is an argument for the pit.

Herman Melville

A good title should aim at making what follows as far as possible superfluous to those who know anything of the subject.

Samuel Butler

It is better to read trash with enjoyment than masterpieces with yawning groans.

Harold Nicolson

[3]

La Russie c'est le néant.

Bismarck

Comme un point fixe fait remarquer l'emportement des autres.

Pascal

An unknown man in a lonely place is a permitted object of fear to a young woman privately bred.

Henry James

Great sorrow never lasts. It is like a stream stemmed — must begin flowing again.

Carlyle

Une ruine est un accident ralenti.

Cocteau

All institutions die of dignity.

Sydney Smith

Children are horribly insecure: the life of a parent is the life of a gambler.

Sydney Smith

I must believe in the Apostolic Succession, there being no other way of accounting for the descent of the Bishop of Exeter from Judas Iscariot.

Sydney Smith

[4]

Characters

Coleridge sat on the brow of Highgate Hill, in those years, looking down on London and its smoke-tumult, like a sage escaped from the inanity of life's battle; attracting towards him the thoughts of innumerable brave souls still engaged there. His express contributions to poetry, philosophy, or any specific province of human literature or enlightenment, had been small and sadly intermittent; but he had, especially among young inquiring men, a higher than literary, a kind of prophetic or magician character. He was thought to hold, he alone in England, the key of German and other Transcendentalisms; knew the sublime secret of believing by 'the reason' what 'the understanding' had been obliged to fling out as incredible; and could still, after Hume and Voltaire had done their best and worst with him, profess himself an orthodox Christian, and say and print to the Church of England, with its singular old rubrics and surplices at Allhallowtide, *Esto perpetua*. A sublime man; who, alone in those dark days, had saved his crown of spiritual manhood; escaping from the black materialisms, and revolutionary deluges, with 'God, Freedom, Immortality' still his: a king of men. The practical intellects of the world did not much heed him, or carelessly reckoned him a metaphysical dreamer: but to the rising spirits of the young generation he had this dusky sublime character; and sat there as a kind of *Magus*, girt in mystery and enigma; his Dodona oak-grove (Mr Gilman's house at Highgate) whispering strange things, uncertain whether oracles or jargon . . .

I have heard Coleridge talk, with eager musical energy, two stricken hours, his face radiant and moist, and communicate no meaning whatsoever to any individual of his hearers, — certain of whom, I for one, still kept eagerly listening in hope; the most had long before given up, and formed (if the room were large enough) secondary humming groups of their own. He began anywhere: you put some question to him, made some suggestive observation; instead of answering this, or decidedly setting out towards answer of it, he would accumulate formidable apparatus, logical swim-bladders, transcendental life-preservers and other precautionary and vehiculatory gear, for setting out; perhaps did at last get under way, — but was swiftly solicited, turned aside by the glance of some radiant new game on this hand or that, into new courses; and ever into new; and before long into all the Universe, where it was uncertain what game you would catch, or whether any . . .

Glorious islets, too, I have seen rise out of the haze; but they were few, and soon swallowed in the general element again. Balmy sunny islets, islets of the blest and the intelligible; — on which occasions those secondary humming groups would all cease humming, and hang breathless upon the eloquent words; till once your islet got wrapt in the mist again, and they could recommence humming. Eloquent artistically expressive words you always had; piercing radiances of a most subtle insight came at intervals; tones of noble pious sympathy, recognisable as pious though strangely coloured, were never wanting long: but in general you could not call this aimless, cloudcapt, cloudbased, lawlessly meandering human discourse of reason by the name of 'excellent talk,' but only of 'surprising;' and were reminded bitterly of Hazlitt's account of it: 'Excellent talker, very, — if you let him start from no premises and come to no conclusion.'

Carlyle

His high rank as an English peer was very injurious to Byron; for every talent is oppressed by the outer world — how much more, then, when there is such high birth and so great a fortune? A middle rank is much more favourable to talent, so we find all great artists and poets in the middle classes. Byron's predilection for the unbounded could not have been nearly so dangerous with more humble birth and smaller means. As it was, he was able to put every fancy into practice, and this involved him in innumerable scrapes. Besides, how could one of such high rank be inspired with awe and respect by any rank whatever? He spoke out whatever he felt, and this brought him into ceaseless conflict with the world.

It is surprising to remark how large a portion of the life of a rich Englishman of rank is passed in duels and elopements. Lord Byron himself says that his father carried off three ladies. And let any man be a steady son after that.

Goethe

Sometimes, if some gentleman saw fit to cross him in anything, he would just stare at him and say 'You swim in shallow water': that was his favourite saying.

Turgenev

Poor Leinster! that man is only about three degrees and a half above a good-tempered Newfoundland dog, and yet I am sorry he is leaving me, perhaps for ever.

Harriette Wilson

While we were conversing together, the young cornet galloped past us: I allude to the one who had been universally cut, ever since he joined, merely, I believe, because no one knew him, and all were certain that his birth was rather mechanical.

Harriette Wilson

Twenty-two acknowledged concubines, and a library of sixty-two thousand volumes, attested the variety of his inclinations; and from the productions which he left behind him, it appears that both the one and the other were designed for use rather than for ostentation.

Gibbon (on the Emperor Gordian)

His father had been something or other in the Treasury; his grandfather, on the mother's side, had been something or other in the Church. He had come into the paternal estate, two or three thousand a year in Hampshire; but he had let the place advantageously and was generous to four ugly sisters who lived at Bournemouth and adored him. The family was hideous all round, but the salt of the earth. He was supposed to be unspeakably clever; he was fond of London, fond of books, of intellectual society and of the idea of a political career. That such a man should be at the same time fond of Flora Saunt attested, as the phrase in the first volume of Gibbon has it, the variety of his inclinations.

Henry James

'I came away more impressed with the fullness of life and energy than with any sense of distinction.'

G. H. Lewes (on first meeting Dickens)

'Don't come flying out of your chair like that, Mr Venus!'
'I ask your pardon, Mr Wegg. I am so soured.'
'Yes, but hang it,' says Mr Wegg argumentatively,
'a well-groomed mind can be soured sitting.'

Dickens

As his character was not good, and he had been bred at a Charity School, in a complete course, according to question and answer, of those ancient people the Amorites and Hittites, he was frequently quoted as an example of the failure of education.

Dickens

'People objected to Professor Dingo, when we were staying in the north of Devon, after our marriage,' said Mrs Badger, 'that he disfigured some of the houses and other buildings by chipping off fragments of those edifices with his little geological hammer. But the Professor replied, that he knew of no building save the Temple of Science. The principle is the same, I think?'
'Precisely the same,' said Mr Badger. 'Finely expressed! The Professor made the same remark, Miss Summerson, in his last illness, when (his mind wandering) he insisted on keeping his little hammer under the pillow, and chipping at the countenances of the attendants. The ruling passion!'

Dickens

In the following year Macaulay died. He was fortunate in the circumstances no less of his death than of his life, for when he ceased to breathe he had the first number of the *Cornhill* open before him, at the first page of Thackeray's *Lovel the Widower.*

Raymond Mortimer

The bowler of Mr Jerome K. Jerome is a perfect preface to all his works. The silk hat of Mr Whistler is a real nocturne, his linen a symphony *en blanc majeur*. To have seen Mr Hall Caine is to have read his soul. His flowing, formless cloak is as one of his own novels, twenty-five editions latent in the folds of it. Melodrama crouches upon the brim of his sombrero. His tie is a Publisher's Announcement. His boots are copyright. In his hand he holds the staff of the *Family Herald.*

Max Beerbohm

Certainly he was a man of a considerable scale. He plodded on from blunder to blunder and from one disaster to another, without losing either the regard of his country or the trust of his troops, to whose feeding as well as to his own he paid serious attention.

Winston Churchill (on Redvers Buller)

Some people said he built too many churches: the only faults *I* found in him were that he thought too highly of mint-sauce, and that he carried his anti-Bonapartism (a thing requiring no excuse in itself) a little too far in respect of the fate of the Prince Imperial.

George Saintsbury (on A. J. B. Beresford-Hope)

[9]

Henry James

Henry James, top hat in hand, important, boring,
Walks beautifully down the long corridor
Of the drowned house just off Dungeness
At the turn of the century. It is 3 p.m. probably.
It is without doubt October. The sun decants
Burgundy through high windows. The family portraits
Are thirteen versions of the one face, walking
On the thick trembling stalk of Henry James.
It is a face which looks like the face of a goldfish
Fed full of breadcrumbs and philosophy, superbly
Reconciled to its bowl. The difference
Between Henry James and a goldfish, however,
Is that Henry James has nostrils. Those nostrils observe
An exquisite scent of evil from the library.
Henry James goes beautifully on his way. His step
Is complicated. (He nurses an obscure hurt. It is this
Which kept him from active service in the sex war.)
Listen and you will hear the trickle of his digestive juices —
Our author has lunched, as usual, well —
Above the sweetly unpleasant hum of his imagination.
His shoes make no squeak and he deposits no shadow
To simplify the carpet. Henry James
Turns a corner. Henry
James meets Henry
James. Top hat, etcetera. Henry James
Stops. Henry James stares. Henry James
Lifts a moral finger. 'You again!'
He sighs. 'How can you be so obvious?'
Henry James blushes and Henry James flees and Henry
James goes beautifully on his way, top hat
In hand, important, boring, he walks down
The long etcetera.

Robert Nye

Seeing them both on the same day — a nice autumn Sunday down at the Cazalets', Fairlawne — and having a chance of being alone with them gives them a good opportunity of contrast.

Kipling at Fairlawne is like a little gnome. All sorts of people about. The Athlones — she with her funny old German governess who says not a word but suddenly breaks out once with 'Ach, Thomas Mann — he's a splendid writer' and looks across the table scornfully at Kipling as though she'd like to tell him how inferior she thinks *he* is. And J. H. Thomas suddenly putting his arm confidentially through mine after lunch, although he scarcely knows me, and chuckling: 'You're a novelist. Well, keep your eye on me, my boy, for I'm your next P.M. 'Ow's that for a prophecy?' And then catching Kipling's arm and chuckling in *his* ear some rather dirty joke about Labour Gentlemen of the Bedchamber. Not that Kipling cares in the least about any of them. He is kindly, genial, ready apparently to be friends with anyone but keeping all the time his own guard.

I asked him at luncheon whether he approved of censorship (a propos of this tiresome stupid *Well of Loneliness*). No, he doesn't approve of the book. Too much of the abnormal in all of us to play about with it. Hates opening up reserves. All the same he'd had friends once and again he'd done more for than for any woman. Luckily Ma Kipling doesn't hear this — but she's had her ear at *his* keyhole for so long that, without hearing anything, she nevertheless suspects and turns her dull eye on to me as much as to say: 'Now the moment you're tiresome you *go*, so if you want to stay with him you'd better behave'. Nor do I blame her. She's a good strong-minded woman, who has played watch-dog to him so long that she knows now just how to save him any kind of disturbance, mental, physical or spiritual. That's *her* job and she does it superbly.

All the same he manages to tell me all about my short stories [*The Silver Thorn*]. He's read them, he really has. Likes especially *The Tarn*. 'By Jove you *are* hard on parsons,' he says and manages to leave a pleasant tingle in my cheeks.

He does this, I fancy, with everyone. He's endlessly kind and endlessly reserved. His black eyebrows, which today jut out like furry rocks over his eyes, keep guard. When I tell him later that we were all amused about his mistake over Jane Austen and Scott,[1] he jokingly defends it, but she doesn't

---

[1] In his poem *Jane's Marriage* Kipling made Sir Walter welcome Jane in Paradise, whereas in fact she died fifteen years before he did. Kipling later revised the poem.

[11]

like my telling him of it and gives me another warning look.

He really, I think, has no vanity. He's a zealous propagandist who, having discovered that the things for which he must propagand are now all out of fashion, guards them jealously and lovingly in his heart, but won't any more trail them about in public.

He walks about the garden, his eyebrows all that are really visible of him. His body is nothing but his eyes terrific, lambent, kindly, gentle and exceedingly proud. Good to us all and we are all shadows to him.

'Carrie,' he says turning to Mrs K, and at once you see that she is the only real person here to him — so she takes him, wraps him up in her bosom and conveys him back to their uncomfortable hard-chaired home. He is quite content.

Winston is quite another matter. 'Tiny' [Victor] Cazalet took me over in the afternoon to his country mansion. I went in some tremor because the times that we've met he has been anything but amiable — grumpy, hunched and silent.

We found him building a wall of a garage at the bottom of the garden. He was in a dirty shirt and brown workman's trousers. He grunted at us and patted his bricks and mortar. Then as he walked up the garden Cazalet told him about Rothermere's labour views. Winston grunted again, muttered: 'Well, what does he *mean* . . . etc, etc.' More of R's views on taxation: 'Yes, we might take it off *beer*. On the other hand . . .' Then suddenly, bringing us opposite a bright pink wall most of which he's built himself, rises to real animation — 'Now *there's* a wall. Beautiful. And it's going to spread as far as this. Nice colour, isn't it? All that I built myself!' Then, his eyes sulky again, grunts once more: 'We might take it off *beer* of course.'

He takes us round the garden and we come to the little lake on which there are some wild-fowl and two black swans majestically floating. Very beautiful, the little lake in the evening faintly green under the shelving lawn, and then ebony black, small pink clouds floating over the wood. He's hugely proud of the two black swans. He calls to them and they, seeing he has no food, move away from him disdainfully. They are as egoistic as he and understand him perfectly. He enjoys their egotism, is fond of them for it.

We move up to the house. I say a few things but he doesn't listen at all, sulky again because he is thinking of Rothermere. Inside the house, which is very pleasant, smells nice, old panelling, dark passages, up in his room he gives me a stiff whisky and soda.

Over his writing-table there is Sargent's drawing of his mother. 'There's a fine thing! She was like that! Wasn't she grand?' He is entirely changed. All the sulkiness is gone. I ask to see his paintings. He's like a schoolboy, shy and

[12]

stiff. Says they are all away, at the bottom of the garden. But they aren't. They are all here stacked behind a bureau. So he drags them out, secretly pleased. And they are alive and interesting, especially some chalk heads. Lots of colour in the skies, Riviera scenes mostly. I praise some and he is entirely modest, saying he's never had time to learn and never will have. And I wonder to myself, would I have seen anything in these if they'd been painted by Mr Snooks of Clapham? Yes, I would. They have vigour, energy, personality. He's like a friendly schoolboy now, not because he likes me but because I've turned his mind to things he's happy about.

He picks up Morley's war apologia and breaks into a flaming account of the war — August 4th incidents. How Morley and Burns, had they waited a day or two, would have been all right, but they wouldn't wait. How Lloyd George nearly waited but just caught the last bus. How he had the Turkish ship confiscated and, if war had been averted, would have certainly been imprisoned for doing so.

Not that he would have cared for prison, you can hear him thinking. He's the real adventurer now and ought to have a cutlass at his belt and a red cap on his head. I like him greatly thus, but he's not very reassuring as a Minister of our dear country. He's the king of the schoolboys and loves to be.

He takes us downstairs to the dining-room where, over the sideboard, he has painted a picture of bottles, glasses and cigar-boxes — a very vibrating lively picture. The bottles greet him as friends.

Then we go. He gives me a friendly goodbye but before I'm in the road he's back into his piratical schemes again.

'Yo ho, Yo ho, and a Bottle of Rum!'

Hugh Walpole

[Enoch Soames]

He was a stooping, shambling person, rather tall, very pale, with longish and brownish hair. He had a thin vague beard — or rather, he had a chin on which a large number of hairs weakly curled and clustered to cover its retreat. He was an odd-looking person; but in the 'nineties odd apparitions were more frequent, I think, than they are now. The young writers of that era — and I was sure this man was a writer — strove earnestly to be distinct in aspect. This man had striven unsuccessfully. He wore a soft black hat of clerical kind but of Bohemian intention, and a grey waterproof cape which, perhaps because it was waterproof, failed to be romantic. I decided that 'dim' was the *mot juste* for him.

Max Beerbohm

[13]

[A Difficult Witness[1]]

Then, to confirm all this, came Mr Frank Holland, who was a difficult witness. An old gentleman, white-haired and shrivelled and deaf and palsied and quavering, he stoutly gave evidence that he had been born in 1883; and there was apparently no mistake about it. Added to this, he was Irish beyond the normal provisions of nature, with the emphasis of art; he might have been one of the Dublin players taking part in a Sean O'Casey play. He also suffered from an eerie form of deafness, the inverse of a banshee's wail; one saw even the baritone of Sir Hartley Shawcross, which is as audible as an actor's voice, come to his ear and be attenuated and disappear into nothingness. Added to that, he had a mind which, in one sense fragile, was in another vigorous. He did not fly off at a tangent — flying things can be brought down — but he crept off at tangents, and not the entire forces of the Central Criminal Court could bring him home. The defending counsel had announced that he was calling Mr Holland to certify that when Michael Joyce was leaving America for England, his passport had arrived after he had left his home in Brooklyn to go down to the steamer, and that Mr Holland had waited to take it from the postman and had carried it down to his friend at a Hoboken pier, and that Mr Holland had then seen it was an American passport. But when the relevant questions were put to the old man, he bridled. They appeared to him to cast aspersions on his gentlemanliness. Yes, he had helped his friend by fetching him his passport, but how was he to know what kind of passport? His attitude sharply indicated that other people might know no better than to be inquisitive, but he had his manners. As the examination went on, old age could be seen shifting itself from the shoulders of Mr Holland to those of the examining counsel; yet Mr Holland contributed enough.

Long ago he had known a girl named Gertrude Emily Brooke. She was called Queenie, he told us, with a sudden affectionate chuckle. She had married a man named Michael Joyce, who worked in America. It was on Michael Joyce's advice that Mr Holland himself had gone to America and followed his calling of civil engineer under the employment of the Pennsylvania Railway Company. He and his wife had seen much of the Joyces in America; they had liked them, and even if they had not, would have been inclined to visit them frequently for the simple reason that they were the only people they knew in New York. And indeed they were lucky to have

[1]In the trial for treason of William Joyce ('Lord Haw-Haw') in 1945.

[14]

friends with such a pleasant home. For the Joyces' house, which has since been reconstructed and is now an estate agent's office, stood on a corner lot in a broad street planted with trees, which is now occupied at one end by Negroes and at the other by Italians, but was then a centre of the Irish community. The German quarter was not far away. He went on to describe how Michael Joyce had told him that he had become an American citizen and advised him to do the same. He took the advice, but came home to England after the outbreak of the First World War; he was greatly inconvenienced by his American citizenship, for he had to register under the Aliens' Act which was passed in 1915 and report all his movements to the police. At this time he had visited Queenie, then settled in Lancashire, and had exchanged commiserations with her, because she was incommoded in the same way. His cracked old voice evoked two people grumbling together thirty years ago. That they had so grumbled could not be doubted.

This witness's evidence recalled the acting of Sir Henry Irving. It was impossible to hear a word of what Irving said for years before he left the stage, and as his memory had gone that was just as well; but the melodic line of his murmurs and the gesture of his gauntness never failed to evoke the truth concerning Shylock, because his intellect possessed that truth and charged such means of expression as still remained to him with instructions to transmit it. Mr Holland was as bewildering a witness as could be imagined. The name of Gertrude Emily Brooke's birthplace, the town of Shaw in Lancashire, inspired him to dazzling feats. Through his deafness he appeared to swear that he had been born there, that he had never been there, that he had seen the Joyces there, and that he had not seen them there, and that he had visited the Joyces in 1919 at a house in which they had in fact settled in 1923. But he had known the Joyces for fifty years; he did recognize the prisoner in the dock as the William Joyce who had been a baby in Herkimer Street, Brooklyn; he had heard Michael Joyce say he was an American and Gertrude Emily Joyce grumble about the necessity to register as an alien; and he was telling the truth. It showed in the irritable twitch of his eyebrows when he was asked to put the truth he knew into a form more likely to convince the jury, the impatient wail of his voice as he made what seemed to him the superfluous repetition. The case against William Joyce, so far as it depended on his British nationality, lay dead on the court-room floor when Mr Holland left the witness-box.

Rebecca West

Condolence

To Miss Grace Norton

July 28th [1883]   *131 Mount Vernon Street, Boston*

My dear Grace, Before the sufferings of others I am always utterly powerless, and your letter reveals such depths of suffering that I hardly know what to say to you. This indeed is not my last word — but it must be my first. You are not isolated, verily, in such states of feeling as this — that is, in the sense that you appear to make all the misery of all mankind your own; only I have a terrible sense that you give all and receive nothing — that there is no reciprocity in your sympathy — that you have all the affliction of it and none of the returns. However — I am determined not to speak to you except with the voice of stoicism. I don't know *why* we live — the gift of life comes to us from I don't know what source or for what purpose; but I believe we can go on living for the reason that (always of course up to a certain point) life is the most valuable thing we know anything about, and it is therefore presumptively a great mistake to surrender it while there is any yet left in the cup. In other words consciousness is an illimitable power, and though at times it may seem to be all consciousness of misery, yet in the way it propagates itself from wave to wave, so that we never cease to feel, and though at moments we appear to, try to, pray to, there is something that holds one in one's place, makes it a standpoint in the universe which it is probably good not to forsake. You are right in your consciousness that we are all echoes and reverberations of the *same*, and you are noble when your interest and pity as to everything that surrounds you, appears to have a sustaining and harmonizing power. Only don't, I beseech you, *generalize* too much in these sympathies and tendernesses — remember that every life is a special problem which is not yours but another's, and content yourself with the terrible algebra of your own. Don't melt too much into the universe, but be as solid and dense and

[16]

fixed as you can. We all live together, and those of us who love and know, live so most. We help each other — even unconsciously, each in our own effort, we lighten the effort of others, we contribute to the sum of success, make it possible for others to live. Sorrow comes in great waves — no one can know that better than you — but it rolls over us, and though it may almost smother us it leaves us on the spot, and we know that if it is strong we are stronger, inasmuch as it passes and we remain. It wears us, uses us, but we wear it and use it in return; and it is blind, whereas we after a manner see. My dear Grace, you are passing through a darkness in which I myself in my ignorance see nothing but that you have been made wretchedly ill by it; but it is only a darkness, it is not an end, or *the* end. Don't think, don't feel, any more than you can help, don't conclude or decide — don't do anything but *wait*. Everything will pass, and serenity and *accepted* mysteries and disillusionments, and the tenderness of a few good people, and new opportunities and ever so much of life, in a word, will remain. You will do all sorts of things yet, and I will help you. The only thing is not to *melt* in the meanwhile. I insist upon the necessity of a sort of mechanical condensation — so that however fast the horse may run away there will, when he pulls up, be a somewhat agitated but perfectly identical G. N. left in the saddle. Try not to be ill — that is all; for in that there is a failure. You are marked out for success, and you must not fail. You have my tenderest affection and all my confidence.   Ever your faithful friend   *Henry James*

Death

Pious spirits who passed their days in raptures of futurity, made little more of this world, than the world that was before it, while they lay obscure in the chaos of pre-ordination, and night of their fore-beings. And if any have been so happy as truly to understand Christian annihilation, ecstasies, exolution, liquefaction, transformation, the kiss of the spouse, gustation of God, and ingression into the divine shadow, they have already had an handsome anticipation of heaven; the glory of the world is surely over, and the earth in ashes unto them.

Sir Thomas Browne

The seas are quiet when the winds give o'er;
So calm are we when passions are no more.
For then we know how vain it was to boast
Of fleeting things, so certain to be lost.
Clouds of affection from our younger eyes
Conceal that emptiness which age descries.

The soul's dark cottage, batter'd and decay'd,
Lets in new light through chinks that Time hath made:
Stronger by weakness, wiser men become
As they draw near to their eternal home.
Leaving the old, both worlds at once they view
That stand upon the threshold of the new.

Edmund Waller

Take away but the pomps of death, the disguises and solemn bugbears, the tinsel, and the actings by candlelight, and proper and fantastic ceremonies, the minstrels and the noise-makers, the women and the weepers, the swoonings and the shriekings, the nurses and the physicians, the dark room and the ministers, the kindred and the watchers; and then to die is easy, ready, and quitted from its troublesome circumstances. It is the same harmless thing that a poor shepherd suffered yesterday, or a maid-servant to-day.

Jeremy Taylor

After Death nothing is, and nothing Death;
The utmost limits of a gasp of breath.
Let the ambitious zealot lay aside
His hopes of heav'n (whose faith is but his pride);
Let slavish souls lay by their fear,
Nor be concerned which way, or where,
After this life we shall be hurl'd:
Dead, we become the lumber of the world;
And to that mass of matter shall be swept,
Where things destroy'd, with things unborn are kept;
Devouring time swallows us whole,
Impartial Death confounds body and soul.
For hell and the foul fiend that rules
The everlasting fiery goals,
Devis'd by rogues, dreaded by fools,
With his grim grizzly dog that keeps the door,
Are senseless stories, idle tales,
Dreams, whimseys, and no more.

Rochester

And eternal delight and deliciousness will be his, who coming to lay him down, can say with his final breath — O Father — chiefly known to me by Thy rod — mortal or immortal, here I die. I have striven to be Thine, more than to be this world's or mine own. Yet this is nothing; I leave eternity to Thee; for what is man that he should live out the lifetime of his God.

Herman Melville

[19]

It often comes into my head
That we may dream when we are dead,
    But I am far from sure we do.
O that it were so! then my rest
Would be indeed among the blest;
    I should for ever dream of you.

Landor

Not till the fire is dying in the grate
Look we for any kinship with the stars.

Meredith

Be near me when my light is low,
    When the blood creeps, and the nerves prick
    And tingle; and the heart is sick,
And all the wheels of Being slow.

Be near me when the sensuous frame
    Is rack'd with pangs that conquer trust;
    And Time, a maniac scattering dust,
And Life, a Fury slinging flame.

Be near me when my faith is dry,
    And men the flies of latter spring,
    That lay their eggs, and sting and sing
And weave their petty cells and die.

Be near me when I fade away,
    To point the term of human strife,
    And on the low dark verge of life
The twilight of eternal day.

Tennyson

Empty grinning apery of commonplace creatures and their loud inanities ought to be more and more shut out from us as the Eternities draw nigh.

Carlyle

Safe in their alabaster chambers,
Untouched by morning and untouched by noon,
Sleep the meek members of the resurrection,
Rafter of satin, and roof of stone.

Light laughs the breeze in her castle of sunshine;
Babbles the bee in a stolid ear;
Pipe the sweet birds in ignorant cadence, —
Ah, what sagacity perished here!

Grand go the years in the crescent above them;
Worlds scoop their arcs, and firmaments row,
Diadems drop and Doges surrender,
Soundless as dots on a disk of snow.

Emily Dickinson

When you to Acheron's ugly water come
Where darkness is and formless mourners brood
And down the shelves of that distasteful flood
Survey the human rank in order dumb,
When the pale dead go forward, tortured more
By nothingness and longing than by fire,
Which bear their hands in suppliance with desire,
With stretched desire for the ulterior shore.

Then go before them like a royal ghost
And tread like Egypt or like Carthage crowned;
Because in your Mortality the most
Of all we may inherit has been found —
    Children for memory: the Faith for pride.
    Good land to leave: and young Love satisfied.

Belloc

Preparing to Leave

Preparing to leave —
attics cleared; shelves and drawers emptied;
love-letters burned and memory purged,
I knew we had always been
preparing to leave.
Those wedding-groups, snaps of childhood,
babyhood, parents — back, back
to the unremembered, thrust
deep into the dust-bin.
The lid clashes louder than the Bible
that life is grass;
possessions rust;
and man a moment of hope
from centuries' dust.

I walk out into wet fields of Spring;
plovers are circling,
crying to the rain and the trees,
calling their young from empty nests —
even these
are pulled away on the swirl and heave
of the wind.
All things that live are preparing to leave.

Phoebe Hesketh

The bustle in a house
The morning after death
Is solemnest of industries
Enacted upon earth, —

The sweeping up the heart,
And putting love away
We shall not want to use again
Until eternity.

Emily Dickinson

[22]

Extracts from Letters

I look upon anecdotes as debts due to the public, which every man, when he has that kind of cash by him, ought to pay.

Lord Orrery to Dr Birch, 1741

I must indeed have slept very fast, not to have been awakened by your letter. None of your suspicions are true; I am not much richer than when you left me; and, what is worse, my omission of an answer to your first letter, will prove that I am not much wiser. But I go on as I formerly did, designing to be some time or other both rich and wise; and yet cultivate neither mind nor fortune. Do you take notice of my example, and learn the danger of delay. When I was as you are now, towering in the confidence of twenty-one, little did I suspect that I should be at forty-nine, what I now am.

Dr Johnson to Bennet Langton, 1758

When Voltaire was asked why no woman has ever written even a tolerable tragedy? 'Ah' (said the Patriarch) 'the composition of a tragedy requires *testicles*.' If this be true, Lord knows what Joanna Baillie does — I suppose she borrows them!

Byron to John Murray, 1817

Dr Polidori has, just now, no more patients, because his patients are no more. He had lately three, who are now all dead — one embalmed. Horner and a child of Thomas Hope's are interred at Pisa and Rome. Lord Guilford died of an inflammation of the bowels: so they took them out, and sent them (on account of their discrepancies), separately from the carcase, to England. Conceive a man going one way, and his intestines another, and his immortal soul a third! — was there ever such a distribution?

Byron to Thomas Moore, 1817

[23]

Nothing can be more disgusting than an Oratorio. How absurd, to see 500 people fiddling like madmen about the Israelites in the Red Sea!

Sydney Smith to Lady Holland, 1823

Such was Blake, as I remember him. He was one of the few to be met with in our passage through life, who are not in some way or other 'double-minded' and inconsistent with themselves; one of the very few who cannot be depressed by neglect, and to whose name rank and station could add no lustre. Moving apart, in a sphere above the attraction of worldly honours, he did not accept greatness, but confer it.

Samuel Palmer to Alexander Gilchrist, 1855[1]

Le néo-catholicisme d'une part et le socialisme de l'autre ont abêti la France. Tout se meurt entre l'Immaculée Conception et les gamelles ouvrières.

Flaubert to George Sand, 1868

I don't think it matters who Christ was as long as one tries to imitate him in his noble life and self-denial.

F. York Powell to E. G. Punchard, 1890

Modern poets take too little trouble to boil down and therefore will perish by the hundreds like jellyfish on the shore; a little gritty shell survives.

F. York Powell to E. G. Punchard, 1890

Wisdom says: do not fill the vacated place — never! This is the only way to a life with phantoms who never perish; who never abandon one; who are always near and depart only when it is time also for yourself to go. I can tell for I have lived during many days with the faithful dead.

Conrad to Edward Garnett, 1897

[1] I copied this out long ago because it immediately reminded me of my beloved Edmund Blunden.

[24]

I went to Genoa to see Constance's grave. It is very pretty — a marble cross with dark ivy-leaves inlaid in a good pattern. The cemetery is a garden at the foot of the lovely hills that climb into the mountains that girdle Genoa. It was very tragic seeing her name carved on a tomb — her surname, my name not mentioned of course — just 'Constance Mary, daughter of Horace Lloyd, Q.C.' and a verse from *Revelations*. I brought some flowers. I was deeply affected — with a sense, also, of the uselessness of all regrets. Nothing could have been otherwise, and Life is a very terrible thing.

Oscar Wilde to Robert Ross, 1899

I am reading Carlyle's *Past and Present.* Curious how stirring and searching his preachment is even while one believes to the bottom of his reason that the man's philosophy of life is hardly worth serious consideration. His literary genius is so great. It illustrates anew the fundamental opposition of poet and philosopher. The man who feels and the man who explains. No man is both in spite of your Goethes.

Mr Justice Holmes to Sir Frederick Pollock, 1899

Our ancestors are thought by many to have had more leisure than we. I don't believe it. They muddled away many hours in doing small things with futile elaboration, and when they were not doing that they took commonplace books and wrote out, as the case might be, extracts from perfectly well known and accessible works, or anecdotes barely worth preserving at all. Women continued this practice longer than men, I think.

Mr Justice Holmes to Sir Frederick Pollock, 1899

I have been reading Schofield on Mediaeval Lit. It makes me cry. These school-boy books, by bright students, won't do. He has not read the books he talks about. He does not authorise his statements of fact. He tries to stun criticism by exhibiting a scrap-heap of machinery. It's all very sad. And if you want to read a book he mentions, he mostly doesn't tell you where it is. His English is sloppy. He was begotten by a thesis on an endowment. He is now teaching pupils how to write worse books of the same kind.

Walter Raleigh to W. P. Ker, 1906

[25]

I think humility is the solution of almost everything. You can't tell whether you have it, till the time comes.

Walter Raleigh to John Sampson, 1906

As I have said so often, all I mean by truth is what I can't help thinking.

Mr Justice Holmes to Sir Frederick Pollock, 1908

I had to remind myself that one should not allow taste to blind one to great qualities, as it is apt to.

Mr Justice Holmes to Sir Frederick Pollock, 1910

Marry your children, sack your servants, forget your enemies, remember your friends, enslave your admirers, fatten yourself — and all will yet be well.

Walter Raleigh to Mrs Dowdall, 1918

I now look forward to what impressed my childhood as most wonderful — to being carried in a civic procession as a survivor. It doesn't matter very much of what.

Mr Justice Holmes to Sir Frederick Pollock, 1919

Mind you don't write any professional English, the garbage of words that conceals lack of thought. 'The development of the poet's individuality constitutes a subject of profound interest' and that sort of thing. Write for Oxford cabmen — in that way you will say more in less space. In most American university books I can't see the fish for the weeds.

Walter Raleigh to Walter Peck, 1920

I was greatly tickled by your account of Arthur Balfour and his pensive solitary session at the café. I fancy his main feeling about Florence must have been 'How wonderful to be here again, after all these years!' When he was eighteen years old he believed that he had certainly not more than three more years to live, and made all his arrangements accordingly. (Oscar Browning, in his book of reminiscences, gives an account of 'that fearful belief' on A.J.B.'s part.) And then, many years later, he found himself being somehow a militant Irish Secretary and feeling a little stronger and better, though still far from well and not at all long for this world. And later on he found himself being Prime Minister for ever so long and exasperating and dominating everybody over the Fiscal Question and feeling decidedly better.

And then came the crash when he lost his seat in Manchester and everybody thought his career was ended because the new Parliament, when he did get returned for another borough, wouldn't listen to him. And presently the new Parliament was sitting at his feet. And then, years later, another crash, and Bonar Law took his place. And then, opportunely, the War; England being a maritime power, Balfour must be at the Admiralty; and then, nobody but Balfour could manage Foreign Affairs; and then, Balfour was the only man whom America would welcome. And now he's President or something of the League of Nations, and constantly improving his stroke in tennis, and is plump without being fat, and has a complexion like a blush-rose, and only one ambition is left to him, who started with no ambition at all and has yet achieved so much; only one ambition (barring the wish to improve still further at tennis), *viz*, to survive *everybody*. I think that perhaps it was the premature death of his old leader Randolph Churchill that first made him feel it was rather a score, as well as a surprise, to be alive. When his juniors, his disciples, began to go — famous athletes, like Alfred Lyttelton, and hidalgos like George Wyndham — and when golden lads like Harry Cust like chimney-sweepers turned to dust, then it was that in the amiable but not very human bosom of A.J.B. there arose a desire to see us *all* laid to rest before his own last hour. I daresay that while he sat sipping his (I am sure) non-alcoholic drink in that Florentine café he was wondering how much longer, down yonder in Rome, that other and greater prodigy, Oscar Browning, was going to go on.

All this sounds very cynical. But it isn't really so. I am convinced that A.J.B. is very cynical. Anyhow, he is a monster. To realise this, you have only to try to conceive that he is, in strict point of fact, an old gentleman. You *can't* conceive that of one who is so like a young lady. So there you are! He used in bygone days to seem rather like one of the dons at Girton; shy in a rather old-maidish way. But now (did I tell you I sat next to him at a men's

[27]

dinner just before I came here in December?) — now he has sloughed whole decades; and the rose-pink flush on those rounded features that were once angular and pale, and a yet softer light in the eyes, and a yet greater timidity and *naiveté* in the manner, make one feel one isn't in the presence of a teacher, but of a recent pupil — a pupil who didn't do so well, either, but had a perfectly heavenly 'time,' at Girton, and would like to be back there, and is as yet rather bewildered by the fuss and glitter of the grown-up world in London, and is especially afraid of dinner-parties, with a man on either side paying compliments, and remembers with a pang of longing those awfully jolly 'feasts' of potted meat and biscuits and jam and bananas in the other girls' studies.

Max Beerbohm to Reggie Turner, 1920

Democracy is about to achieve its greatest triumph. Harding, I hear, will be elected by a colossal plurality. He is almost the ideal President. He looks like a somewhat decayed moving-picture actor, belongs to all the secret orders that plumbers and garbage-haulers belong to, and can scarcely speak intelligible English. Mr Malaprop in the White House, vice the Presbyterian Jesus, retired.[1] I shall vote for him.

H. L. Mencken to Hugh Walpole, 1921

What a divine gift is fire. In the clearing up that I have nearly finished I have cut short a thousand hesitations and shut out many fool vistas of possible interest by burning odds and ends. Civilisation is the process of reducing the infinite to the finite.

Mr Justice Holmes to Sir Frederick Pollock, 1922

[1] Woodrow Wilson, of whom Clemenceau said: '*Il parle comme Jésus-Christ, mais il se conduit comme Lloyd George.*'

[28]

Fun

Dolores replies to Swinburne

Cold passions, and perfectly cruel,
    Long odes that go on for an hour,
With a most economical jewel
    And a quite metaphorical flower.
I implore you to stop it and stow it,
    I adjure you, relent and refrain,
Oh, pagan Priapean poet,
                 You give me a pain.

I am sorry, old dear, if I hurt you,
    No doubt it is all very nice
With the lilies and languours of virtue
    And the raptures and roses of vice.
But the notion impels me to anger,
    That vice is all rapture for me,
And if you think virtue is languour
             Just try it and see.

We shall know what the critics discover
    If your poems were shallow or deep,
Who read you from cover to cover,
    Will know if they sleep not or sleep.
But you say I've endured through the ages
    (Which is rude) as Our Lady of Pain,
You have said it for several pages,
             So say it again.

Chesterton

[29]

Confusion

Dear Beachcomber, Life in a Government office is very odd in time of war. Yesterday a young man with untidy red hair dashed into my room and asked, 'Where are the estimates?' 'What estimates?' I asked. 'Yesterday's,' said he. This was all Greek to me. He then said that Gumbrill had told him to collect them. I had never heard of Gumbrill, and I had no estimates, so I said, 'Who are you?' 'Waterton, of course,' said he. 'Why "of course"?' I asked. 'It doesn't follow. You might be any one.' 'I might be,' he said, 'but I'm not.' 'Not what?' I asked. 'Waterton,' he said, 'or rather, any one, I mean. I *am* Waterton, as I said.' 'Well, I'm Thake,' I said. 'I know,' he answered. 'But,' said I, 'I know nothing of all this.' 'Wrong department, then,' said he, and dashed out. I asked my secretary what it was all about, but she didn't know. Later another man came in and said he was Gumbrill, and that it was a mistake. He had thought I was Thake. 'But I am,' said I. 'Oh,' said he, 'Then I don't understand.' 'Nor do I,' said I, 'so let's leave it at that.' Which we did. Yours ever, O. THAKE

Beachcomber (J. B. Morton)

Ten year-old child's essay on 'Describe a bird or an animal'

The bird I am going to write about is the owl. The owl cannot see by day, and at night is as blind as a bat. I do not know much about the owl so I will go on to the beast which I am going to choose. It is the cow. The cow is a mammal. It has six sides — right, left, an upper and below. At the back it has a tail on which hangs a brush. With this it sends the flies away so that they do not fall into the milk. The head is for the purpose of growing horns and so that the mouth can be somewhere. The horns are to butt with and the mouth is to moo with. Under the cow hangs the milk. It is arranged for milking. When people milk, the milk comes and there is no end to the supply. How the cow does it I have not yet realised, but it makes more and more. The cow has a fine sense of smell. One can smell it far away this is the reason for the fresh air in the country.

The male cow is called an ox. It is not a mammal. The cow doesn't eat much, but what it eats it eats twice so that it gets enough. When it is hungry it moos, and when it says nothing it is because its inside is all full up with grass.

Bus Fuss

Item for collectors of war-time transport stories is brought to London by an R.A.F. man on leave from a Lancashire camp.

The other morning, he says, he and his friends scrambled on a bus during the rush hour. The clippie counted, then said: 'There's one too many — somebody will have to get off.' Nobody moved. 'If the last one doesn't get off,' she shouted, 'I'll call the driver.'

Round came the driver. 'I'll call the police if somebody doesn't get out of it,' he said.

Nobody did, so the driver and clippie went off in search of a policeman.

Meantime a meek, bowler-hatted little fellow walked up, boarded the bus, ignored by the other passengers.

A few moments later, the driver, the clippie and the policeman appeared. 'This bus,' threatened the policeman, 'won't move till one gets off.'

Off got the bowler-hatted fellow. 'And why could not you do it before?' asked the clippie angrily, signalling the bus to start. Gusts of laughter from the R.A.F. men, which so rattled the clippie that she stopped the bus a second time. 'This bus won't go while you laugh at me,' she announced.

By this time another bus, with an inspector aboard, had drawn up behind. Inspector asked, 'What on earth's all the trouble?' and, being told by the clippie that everybody was laughing at her, he said, 'In that case you had better change places with the conductress in the other bus.'

New clippie, very businesslike, came forward. Just as she was reaching for the bell-push to get the bus away she noticed the bowler-hatted fellow still waiting by the stop.

'Do you want this bus?' she asked. 'Well, for heaven's sake come along then. We can't hang about all day.'

(Daily paper 1945)

The Lord's Prayer contains 56 words, the Ten Commandments 297, the American Declaration of Independence 300. The European Economic Community Directive on the Export of Duck Eggs contains 26,911 words.

Sunday Express, December 1977

A Birthday Card from William Plomer

"Sleepy?"

"Mmm."

"I believe they put tranquillizers in the sherbet."

"Mmm."

"Who'd have thought that a cheap tourist night-flight by Circassian Airways could be so restful?"

"Mmm."

"It's these _divine_ Pneumofoam Bouncisponge Couchettes."

"Mmm."

"But it's a bit crowded. When I turn, you'll have to turn, so will Ayesha, so will Zuleika, Selina, Lalla Rookh, Pamela Hansford Johnson, Margharita Laski (they seem to be _everywhere_, those two), & the whole bunch."

"Mmm."

"Do you know whose birthday it is tomorrow?"

"Mmm."

"Aren't you going to send him a wish?"

"Mmmmm. Dear Rupert! Many, many happies!"

Immensity

If some king of the earth have so large an extent of dominion, in north and south, as that he hath winter and summer together in his dominions, so large an extent, east and west, as that he hath day and night together in his dominions, much more hath God mercy and judgment together: He brought light out of darkness, not out of a lesser light; He can bring thy summer out of winter, though thou have no spring: though in the ways of fortune or understanding, or conscience, thou have been benighted till now, wintered and frozen, clouded and eclipsed, damped and benumbed, smothered and stupefied till now, — now God comes to thee, not as in the dawning of the day, not as in the bud of the spring, but as the sun at noon to illustrate all shadows, as the sheaves in harvest to fill all penuries: all occasions invite His mercies, and all times are His seasons.

Donne

Incidents

[The Eve of the Battle of Dunbar]

And so the soldiers stand to their arms, or lie within instant reach of their arms, all night; being upon an engagement very difficult indeed. The night is wild and wet; — 2nd of September means 12th by our calendar: the Harvest Moon wades deep among clouds of sleet and hail. Whoever has a heart for prayer, let him pray now, for the wrestle of death is at hand. Pray, — and withal keep his powder dry! And be ready for extremities, and quit himself like a man! — Thus they pass the night; making that Dunbar Peninsula and Brock Rivulet long memorable to me. We English have some tents; the Scots have none. The hoarse sea moans bodeful, swinging low and heavy against these whinstone bays; the sea and the tempests are abroad, all else asleep but we, — and there is One that rides on the wings of the wind.

Carlyle

[The Fall of the Bastille]

O evening sun of July, how, at this hour, thy beams fall slant on reapers amid peaceful woody fields; on old women spinning in cottages; on ships far out in the silent main; on Balls at the Orangerie of Versailles, where high-rouged Dames of the Palace are even now dancing with double-jacketed Hussar-Officers; — and also on this roaring Hell-porch of a Hôtel-de-Ville! Babel Tower, with the confusion of tongues, were not Bedlam added with the conflagration of thoughts, was no type of it. One forest of distracted steel bristles, endless, in front of an Electoral Committee; points itself, in horrid radii, against this and the other accused breast. It was the Titans warring with Olympus; and they, scarcely crediting it, have *conquered*: prodigy of prodigies; delirious, — as it could not but be. Denunciation, vengeance; blaze of triumph on a dark ground of terror: all outward, all inward things fallen into one general wreck of madness!

Carlyle

[35]

Midnight on the Great Western

In the third-class seat sat the journeying boy,
     And the roof-lamp's oily flame
Played down on his listless form and face,
Bewrapt past knowing to what he was going,
          Or whence he came.

In the band of his hat the journeying boy
     Had a ticket stuck; and a string
Around his neck bore the key of his box,
That twinkled gleams of the lamp's sad beams
          Like a living thing.

What past can be yours, O journeying boy
     Towards a world unknown,
Who calmly, as if indifferent quite
To all at stake, can undertake
          This plunge alone?

Knows your soul a sphere, O journeying boy,
     Our rude realms far above,
Whence with spacious vision you mark and mete
This region of sin that you find you in
          But are not of?

Hardy

I always say you can get your tragedy of any desired length in England, from thirty seconds to a life-time. I had one adorable one of twenty-nine minutes by the watch. At the end of that time I started for my train. Woman I'd had a glimpse of in London — walk. She sat on a stile, I below her, gazing into her eyes — then, 'remember this lane,' 'while memory holds its seat etc'. 'Adieu.' And I still do and ever shall remember her, and I rather think she does me a little bit. What imbecilities for an old fellow to be talking. But if one knows his place and makes way for younger men when he isn't sure, it is better perhaps not quite to abandon interest in the sports of life.

Mr Justice Holmes

The Portrait

Midnight past! Not a sound of aught
   Thro' the silent house, but the wind at his prayers.
I sat by the dying fire, and thought
   Of the dear dead woman upstairs.

A night of tears! for the gusty rain
   Had ceased, but the eaves were dripping yet;
And the moon look'd forth, as tho' in pain,
   With her face all white and wet.

Nobody with me, my watch to keep,
   But the friend of my bosom, the man I love:
And grief had sent him fast to sleep
   In the chamber up above.

Nobody else, in the country place
   All round, that knew of my loss beside,
But the good young Priest with the Raphael-face,
   Who confess'd her when she died.

That good young Priest is of gentle nerve,
   And my grief had moved him beyond control;
For his lip grew white, as I could observe,
   When he speeded her parting soul.

I sat by the dreary hearth alone:
   I thought of the pleasant days of yore:
I said 'the staff of my life is gone:
   The woman I loved is no more.

'On her cold, dead bosom my portrait lies,
   Which next to her heart she used to wear —
Haunting it o'er with her tender eyes
   When my own face was not there.

'It is set all round with rubies red,
   And pearls which a Peri might have kept.
For each ruby there, my heart hath bled:
   For each pearl, my eyes have wept.'

And I said — 'the thing is precious to me:
   They will bury her soon in the churchyard clay;
It lies on her heart, and lost must be,
   If I do not take it away.'

I lighted my lamp at the dying flame,
    And crept up the stairs that creak'd for fright,
Till into the chamber of death I came,
    Where she lay all in white.

The moon shone over her winding sheet.
    There, stark she lay on her carven bed:
Seven burning tapers about her feet,
    And seven about her head.

As I stretch'd my hand, I held my breath;
    I turn'd as I drew the curtains apart:
I dared not look on the face of death:
    I knew where to find her heart,

I thought, at first, as my touch fell there,
    It had warm'd that heart to life, with love;
For the thing I touched was warm, I swear,
    And I could feel it move.

'Twas the hand of a man, that was moving slow
    O'er the heart of the dead, — from the other side:
And at once the sweat broke over my brow,
    'Who is robbing the corpse?' I cried.

Opposite me, by the tapers' light,
    The friend of my bosom, the man I loved,
Stood over the corpse, and all as white,
    And neither of us moved.

'What do you here my friend?' . . . The man
    Look'd first at me, and then at the dead.
'There is a portrait here' he began;
    'There is. It is mine,' I said.

Said the friend of my bosom, 'Yours, no doubt,
    The portrait was, till a month ago,
When this suffering angel took that out,
    And placed mine there, I know.'

'This woman, she loved me well,' said I.
    'A month ago,' said my friend to me:
'And in your throat,' I groan'd, 'you lie!'
    He answer'd . . . 'Let us see.'

'Enough!' I return'd, 'let the dead decide:
    And whose soever the portrait prove,
His shall it be, when the cause is tried,
    Where Death is arraign'd by Love.'

We found the portrait there, in its place:
    We open'd it by the tapers' shine:
The gems were all unchanged: the face
    Was — neither his nor mine.

'One nail drives out another, at least!
    The face of the portrait there,' I cried,
'Is our friend's, the Raphael-faced young Priest,
    Who confess'd her when she died.'

The setting is all of rubies red,
    And pearls which a Peri might have kept.
For each ruby there my heart hath bled:
    For each pearl my eyes have wept.

Owen Meredith (Robert, first Earl of Lytton)

My Sister's Sleep

She fell asleep on Christmas Eve:
    At length the long-ungranted shade
    Of weary eyelids overweigh'd
The pain nought else might yet relieve.

Our mother, who had leaned all day
    Over the bed from chime to chime,
    Then raised herself for the first time,
And as she sat her down, did pray.

Her little work-table was spread
    With work to finish. For the glare
    Made by her candle, she had care
To work some distance from the bed.

Without, there was a cold moon up,
    Of winter radiance sheer and thin;
    The hollow halo it was in
Was like an icy crystal cup.

Through the small room, with subtle sound
  Of flame, by vents the fireshine drove
  And reddened. In its dim alcove
The mirror shed a clearness round.

I had been sitting up some nights,
  And my tired mind felt weak and blank;
  Like a sharp strengthening wine it drank
The stillness and the broken lights.

Twelve struck. That sound, by dwindling years
  Heard in each hour, crept off; and then
  The ruffled silence spread again,
Like water that a pebble stirs.

Our mother rose from where she sat:
  Her needles, as she laid them down,
  Met lightly, and her silken gown
Settled: no other noise than that.

'Glory unto the Newly Born!'
  So, as said angels, she did say;
  Because we were in Christmas Day,
Though it would still be long till morn.

Just then in the room over us
  There was a pushing back of chairs,
  As some who had sat unawares
So late, now heard the hour, and rose.

With anxious softly-stepping haste
  Our mother went where Margaret lay,
  Fearing the sounds o'erhead — should they
Have broken her long watched-for rest!

She stopped an instant, calm, and turned;
  But suddenly turned back again;
  And all her features seemed in pain
With woe, and her eyes gazed and yearned.

For my part, I but hid my face,
  And held my breath, and spoke no word:
  There was none spoken; but I heard
The silence for a little space.

Our mother bowed herself and wept:
    And both my arms fell, and I said,
    'God knows I knew that she was dead.'
And there, all white, my sister slept.

Then kneeling, upon Christmas morn
    A little after twelve o'clock
    We said, ere the first quarter struck,
'Christ's blessing on the newly born!'

D. G. Rossetti

Lorraine Lorraine Lorree

Are you ready for your steeple-chase, Lorraine, Lorraine, Lorree?
    Barum, Barum, Barum, Barum, Barum, Barum, Baree.
You're booked to ride your capping race to-day at Coulterlee,
You're booked to ride Vindictive, for all the world to see,
To keep him straight, and keep him first, and win the run for me.
    Barum, Barum, Barum, Barum, Barum, Barum, Baree.

She clasped her new-born baby, poor Lorraine, Lorraine, Lorree.
    Barum, Barum, Barum, Barum, Barum, Barum, Baree.
I cannot ride Vindictive, as any man might see.
And I will not ride Vindictive, with this baby on my knee;
He's killed a boy, he's killed a man, and why must he kill me?

Unless you ride Vindictive, Lorraine, Lorraine, Lorree,
Unless you ride Vindictive to-day at Coulterlee,
And land him safe across the brook and win the race for me,
It's you may keep your baby, for you'll get no help from me.

That husbands could be cruel, said Lorraine, Lorraine, Lorree,
That husbands could be cruel, I have known for seasons three;
But oh! to ride Vindictive while a baby cries for me,
And be killed across a fence at last for all the world to see!

She mastered young Vindictive — Oh! the gallant lass was she,
And kept him straight and won the race as near as near could be;
But he killed her at the brook against a pollard willow tree,
Oh! he killed her at the brook, the brute, for all the world to see.
And no one but the baby cried for poor Lorraine, Lorree.

Charles Kingsley[1]

[1]My mother used to recite this to me when I was very young, and I could never hear it often enough.

The Toys

My little Son, who look'd from thoughtful eyes,
And moved and spoke in quiet grown-up wise,
Having my law the seventh time disobey'd,
I struck him, and dismiss'd
With hard words and unkiss'd,
His Mother, who was patient, being dead.
Then, fearing lest his grief should hinder sleep,
I visited his bed,
But found him slumbering deep,
With darken'd eyelids, and their lashes yet
From his late sobbing wet.
And I, with moan,
Kissing away his tears, left others of my own;
For, on a table drawn beside his head,
He had put, within his reach,
A box of counters and a red-vein'd stone,
A piece of glass abraded by the beach,
And six or seven shells,
A bottle with bluebells,
And two French copper coins, ranged there with careful art,
To comfort his sad heart.
So, when that night I pray'd
To God, I wept, and said:
Ah, when at last we lie with tranced breath,
Not vexing Thee in death,
And Thou rememberest of what toys
We made our joys,
How weakly understood,
Thy great commanded good,
Then, fatherly not less
Than I whom Thou hast moulded from the clay,
Thou'lt leave Thy wrath, and say,
'I will be sorry for their childishness.'

Coventry Patmore

[42]

Near Lanivet, 1872

There was a stunted handpost just on the crest,
    Only a few feet high:
She was tired, and we stopped in the twilight-time for her rest,
    At the crossways close thereby.

She leant back, being so weary, against its stem,
    And laid her arms on its own,
Each open palm stretched out to each end of them,
    Her sad face sideways thrown.

Her white-clothed form at this dim-lit cease of day
    Made her look as one crucified
In my gaze at her from the midst of the dusty way,
    And hurriedly 'Don't,' I cried.

I do not think she heard. Loosing thence she said,
    As she stepped forth ready to go,
'I am rested now. — Something strange came into my head;
    I wish I had not leant so!'

And wordless we moved onward down from the hill
    In the west cloud's murked obscure,
And looking back we could see the handpost still
    In the solitude of the moor.

'It struck her too,' I thought, for as if afraid
    She heavily breathed as we trailed;
Till she said, 'I did not think how 'twould look in the shade,
    When I leant there like one nailed.'

I, lightly: 'There's nothing in it. For *you*, anyhow!'
    — 'O I know there is not,' said she . . .
'Yet I wonder . . . If no one is bodily crucified now.
    In spirit one may be!'

And we dragged on and on, while we seemed to see
    In the running of Time's far glass
Her crucified, as she had wondered if she might be
    Some day. — Alas, alas!

                                                            Hardy[1]

[1] My friend the poet Andrew Young could not read this poem without weeping.

[Wagner Conducting]

Herr Richter's popularity as an orchestral conductor began, not in the auditorium, but in the orchestra. It dates from his first visit here in 1877 to conduct the Wagner festivals at the Albert Hall. At these concerts there was a large and somewhat clumsy band of about 170 players, not well accustomed to the music, and not at all accustomed to the composer, who had contracted to heighten the sensation by conducting a portion of each concert. It is not easy to make an English orchestra nervous, but Wagner's tense neuralgic glare at the players as they waited for the beat with their bows poised above the strings was hard upon the sympathetic men, whilst the intolerable length of the pause exasperated the tougher spirits. When all were effectually disconcerted, the composer's *bâton* was suddenly jerked upwards, as if by a sharp twinge of gout in his elbow; and, after a moment of confusion, a scrambling start was made. During the performance Wagner's glare never relaxed: he never looked pleased. When he wanted more emphasis he stamped; when the division into bars was merely conventional he disdained counting, and looked daggers — spoke them too, sometimes — at innocent instrumentalists who were enjoying the last few bars of their rest without any suspicion that the impatient composer had just discounted half a stave or so and was angrily waiting for them. When he laid down the *bâton* it was with the air of a man who hoped he might never be condemned to listen to such a performance again. Then Herr Richter stepped into the conductor's desk; and the orchestra, tapping their desks noisily with their bows, revenged themselves by an ebullition of delight and deep relief, which scandalized Wagner's personal admirers, but which set the fashion of applauding the new conductor, whose broad, calm style was doubly reassuring after that of Wagner. He, meanwhile, sat humbly among the harps until he could no longer bear to listen quietly to his own music, when he would rise, get into the way of the players, seek flight by no thoroughfares and return discomfited, to escape at last into the stalls and prowl from chair to chair like a man lost and friendless. As it is difficult to remain in the room with the greatest living composer without watching his movements, even at the risk of missing some of his music — which, after all, you will have other chances of hearing — you perhaps paid less attention to Herr Richter than he deserved.

Shaw

Santorin

(A Legend of the Aegean)

'Who are you, Sea Lady,
And where in the seas are we?
I have too long been steering
By the flashes in your eyes.
Why drops the moonlight through my heart,
And why so quietly
Go the great engines of my boat
As if their souls were free?'
'Oh ask me not, bold sailor;
Is not your ship a magic ship
That sails without a sail:
Are not these isles the Isles of Greece
And dust upon the sea?
But answer me three questions
And give me answers three.
What is your ship?' 'A British.'
'And where may Britain be?'
'Oh it lies north, dear lady;
It is a small country.'
'Yet you will know my lover,
Though you live far away:
And you will whisper where he has gone,
That lily boy to look upon
And whiter than the spray.'
'How should I know your lover,
Lady of the sea?'
'Alexander, Alexander,
The King of the World was he.'
'Weep not for him, dear lady,
But come aboard my ship.
So many years ago he died,
He's dead as dead can be.'
'O base and brutal sailor
To lie this lie to me.
His mother was the foam-foot
Star-sparkling Aphrodite;

His father was Adonis
Who lives away in Lebanon,
In stony Lebanon, where blooms
His red anemone.
But where is Alexander,
The soldier Alexander,
My golden love of olden days
The King of the World and me?'

She sank into the moonlight
And the sea was only sea.

Flecker

Travelling to my second Marriage on the Day of the First Moonshot

We got into the carriage. It was hot.
An old woman sat there, her white hair
Stained at the temples as if by smoke.
Beside her the old man, her husband,
Talking of salmon, grayling, sea-trout, pike,
Their ruined waters.

A windscreen wiper on another engine
Flickered like an irritable, a mad eyelid.
The woman's mouth fell open. She complained.
Her husband said: 'I'd like
A one-way ticket to the moon.
Wouldn't mind that.'

'What for?' 'Plant roses.' '*Roses?*' 'Roses,
Yes. I'd be the first rose-grower on the moon.
Mozart, I'd call my rose. That's it.
A name for a new rose: Mozart.
That's what I'd call the first rose on the moon,
If I got there to grow it.'

Ten nine eight seven six five four three two one.
The old woman, remember her, and the old man:
Her black shoes tapping; his gold watch as he counted.
They'd been to a funeral. We were going to a wedding.
When the train started the wheels sang *Figaro*
And there was a smell of roses.

Robert Nye

The Planes of Bedford Square

Never were the plane trees loftier, leafier,
the planes of Bedford Square,
and of all that summer foliage motionless
not one leaf
had fallen yet, one afternoon
warm in the last world-peace before
the First World War.

At Number Thirty, consulate
of the very last Czar,
before a window on the tall first floor
Baron H., the consul, dreamy
with a Flor de Dindigul cigar,
saw the slow smoke
ghosting an arboreal form.

Tennis was thudding underneath the trees
on grass close-shorn.
A quick racquet flashed
the thump of a return,
and a young voice called the score
as if all was for the best
everywhere, not only on this marked-out lawn.

And all the soaring trees, a tree-of-heaven among them,
wore their enormous shawls of leaves
in full dress, over the court, over
the railed-in shade. Not one leaf,
not one, was yet to fall. On the first floor
was there yet one thought, one
forethought of compulsive and appalling war?

Firbank had started carving hardstone
tesserae to fit his semi-precious prose,
had fondly made a bishop's daughter yearn
'Oh, I could dance for ever
to the valse from *Love Fifteen*!',
foresaw perhaps that she might burn
to ash without one invitation to a ball.

[47]

In this well-ordered square the front door yawned
of Number Forty-Four,
and slowly into sunlight sailed
Lady Ottoline, *en grande tenue*, holding herself
as proudly as a rare goose swims;
she was swimming away from the grand and dull,
herself, as ever, too grand to conform.

On her right, the alertest of profiles
fronted the best of brains; her long-boned hand
rested on Bertrand Russell's arm.
On her left, poised on legs
without precedent, Nijinsky himself —
poised as if he could prance for ever
without a thought of any curtain-fall.

Nijinsky, seeing the ballet
of tennis players in white
darting between the tall, theatrical
and sepia-mottled columns of the vaulting trees,
threw out a dancer's arm, and called
in a faun's warm voice
'Ah, quel décor!'

The ball slapped into the net. It made the score
a dangerous deuce. A long white ash
dropped from the Baron's cigar. Peace hives
the virus of war. 'Game! And set!'
That moment under the plane trees (*quel décor!*)
was what these lines were cast to recall,
a crystal moment that seemed worth trawling for.

William Plomer

Fighting [in North Africa in December 1940] continued all day, and by
ten o'clock the Coldstream [Third] Battalion headquarters signalled that it
was impossible to count the prisoners on account of their numbers, but that
there were 'about five acres of officers and two hundred acres of other ranks'.

Winston Churchill

Johnson

I found him buffeting his books, as upon a former occasion, covered with dust.

Boswell

No place affords a more striking conviction of the vanity of human hopes than a public library.

Sir, he [F. Lewis] lived in London, and hung loose upon society.

Jones loved beer, and did not get very forward in the Church.

The expectation of ignorance is indefinite and that of knowledge is often tyrannical. It is hard to satisfy those who know not what to demand when they unite with those who demand what they know is impossible to be done.

I am not yet so lost in lexicography as to forget that words are the daughters of earth, and that things are the sons of heaven.

To adjust the minute events of literary history is tedious and troublesome; it requires indeed no great force of understanding, but often depends upon enquiries which there is no opportunity of making, or is to be fetched from books and pamphlets not always at hand.

Those are no proper judges of his [Savage's] conduct who have slumbered away their time on the down of plenty.

His [Prior's] phrases are original, but they are sometimes harsh; as he inherited no elegances, none has he bequeathed. His expression has every mark of laborious study; the line seldom seems to have been formed at once; the words did not come till they were called, and were then put by constraint into their places, where they do their duty, but do it sullenly.

Thus for *Boswell's Life of Johnson* has Time done, is Time still doing, what no ornament of Art or Artifice could have done for it. Rough Samuel and sleek wheedling James *were*, and *are not*. Their Life and whole personal Environment has melted into air. The Mitre Tavern still stands in Fleet Street: but where now is its scot-and-lot paying, beef-and-ale loving, cocked-hatted, pot-bellied Landlord; its rosy-faced assiduous Landlady, with all her shining brass-pans, waxed tables, well-filled larder-shelves; her cooks, and bootjacks, and errand-boys, and watery-mouthed hangers-on? Gone! Gone! The becking waiter who, with wreathed smiles, was wont to spread for Samuel and Bozzy their supper of the gods, has long since pocketed his last sixpence; and vanished, sixpences and all, like a ghost at cock-crowing. The Bottles they drank out of are all broken, the Chairs they sat on all rotted and burnt; the very Knives and Forks they ate with have rusted to the heart, and become brown oxide of iron, and mingled with the indiscriminate clay. All, all has vanished; in very deed and truth, like that baseless fabric of Prospero's air-vision. Of the Mitre Tavern nothing but the bare walls remain there: of London, of England, of the World, nothing but the bare walls remain; and

[50]

these also decaying (were they of adamant), only slower. The mysterious River of Existence rushes on: a new Billow thereof has arrived, and lashes wildly as ever round the old embankments; but the former Billow with *its* loud, mad eddyings, where is it? — Where! — Now this Book of Boswell's, this is precisely a revocation of the edict of Destiny; so that Time shall not utterly, not so soon by several centuries, have dominion over us. A little row of Naphtha-lamps, with its line of Naphtha-light, burns clear and holy through the dead Night of the Past: they who are gone are still here; though hidden they are revealed, though dead they yet speak. There it shines, that little miraculously lamplit Pathway; shedding its feebler and feebler twilight into the boundless dark Oblivion, — for all that our Johnson *touched* has become illuminated for us: on which miraculous little Pathway we can still travel, and see wonders.

Carlyle

Leaving now this our English *Odyssey,* with its Singer and Scholiast, let us come to the *Ulysses*; that great Samuel Johnson himself, the far-experienced, 'much-enduring man,' whose labours and pilgrimage are here sung. A full-length image of his Existence has been preserved for us: and he, perhaps of all living Englishmen, was the one who best deserved that honour. For if it is true, and now almost proverbial, that 'the Life of the lowest mortal, if faithfully recorded, would be interesting to the highest;' how much more when the mortal in question was already distinguished in fortune and natural quality, so that his thinkings and doings were not significant of himself only, but of large masses of mankind!

Carlyle

Quite spotless, on the other hand, is Johnson's love of Truth, if we look at it as expressed in Practice, as what we have named Honesty of action. 'Clear your mind of Cant;' *clear* it, throw Cant utterly away: such was his emphatic, repeated precept; and did not he himself faithfully conform to it? The Life of this man has been, as it were, turned inside out, and examined with microscopes by friend and foe; yet was there no Lie found in him. His Doings

[51]

and Writings are not *shows* but *performances*: you may weigh them in the balance, and they will stand weight. Not a line, not a sentence is dishonestly done, is other than it pretends to be. Alas! and he wrote not out of inward inspiration, but to earn his wages: and with that grand perennial tide of 'popular delusion' flowing by; in whose waters he nevertheless refused to fish, to whose rich oyster-beds the dive was too muddy for him. Observe, again, with what innate hatred of Cant, he takes for himself, and offers to others, the lowest possible view of his business, which he followed with such nobleness. Motive for writing he had none, as he often said, but money; and yet he wrote *so*. Into the region of Poetic Art he indeed never rose; there was no *ideal* without him avowing itself in his work: the nobler was that unavowed *ideal* which lay within him, and commanded saying, Work out thy Artisanship in the spirit of an Artist!

Carlyle

To Samuel Johnson, LL.D.

Dear Sir, By inscribing this slight performance [*She Stoops to Conquer*] to you, I do not mean so much to compliment you as myself. It may do me some honour to inform the public, that I have lived many years in intimacy with you. It may serve the interests of mankind also to inform them, that the greatest wit may be found in a character, without impairing the most unaffected piety.

Goldsmith

Johnson marched to kettle-drums and trumpets; Gibbon moved to flutes and hautboys: Johnson hewed passages through the Alps, while Gibbon levelled walks through parks and gardens.

George Colman the Younger

Landor

Stand close around, ye Stygian set,
   With Dirce in one boat convey'd!
Or Charon, seeing, may forget
   That he is old and she a shade.

Authors should never be seen by authors, and little by other people. The Dalai Lama is a god to the imagination, a child to the sight; and a poet is much the same.

The very beautiful rarely love at all. Those precious images are placed above the reach of the Passions: Time alone is permitted to efface them; Time, the father of the Gods, and even *their* consumer.

Study is the bane of boyhood, the aliment of youth, the indulgence of manhood, and the restorative of old age.

A poet often does more and better than he is aware at the time, and seems at last to know as little about it as a silkworm about the fineness of her thread.

'Do you remember me? or are you proud?'
Lightly advancing thro' her star-trimm'd crowd,
    Ianthe said, and look'd into my eyes.
'A *yes,* a *yes* to both: for memory
Where you but once have been must ever be,
And at your voice Pride from his throne must rise.'

He who is within two paces of the ninetieth year may sit down and make no excuses; he must be unpopular, he never tried to be much otherwise; he never contended with a contemporary, but walked alone on the far eastern uplands, meditating and remembering.

We often hear that such or such a thing 'is not worth an old song'. Alas! how very few things are!

Love always makes us better, Religion sometimes, Power never.

Laodameia died; Helen died; Leda, the beloved of Jupiter, went before. It is better to repose in the earth betimes than to sit up late; better, than to cling pertinaciously to what we feel crumbling under us, and to protract an inevitable fall. We may enjoy the present while we are insensible of infirmity and decay: but the present, like a note in music, is nothing but as it appertains to what is past and what is to come. There are no fields of amaranth on this side of the grave; there are no voices, O Rhodope, that are not soon mute, however tuneful; there is no name, with whatever emphasis of passionate love repeated, of which the echo is not faint at last.

The leaves are falling; so am I;
The few late flowers have moisture in the eye;
 So have I too.
Scarcely on any bough is heard
Joyous, or even unjoyous, bird
 The whole wood through.
Winter may come: he brings but nigher
His circle (yearly narrowing) to the fire
 Where old friends meet:
Let him; now heaven is overcast
And spring and summer both are past,
 And all things sweet.

We hurry to the river we must cross,
 And swifter downward every footstep wends;
Happy who reach it ere they count the loss
 Of half their faculties and half their friends!

If anything could engage me to visit Rome again, to endure the sight of her
scarred and awful ruins, telling their stories on the ground in the midst of
bellrings and pantomimes; if I could let charnel-houses and opera-houses,
consuls and popes, tribunes and cardinals, senatorial orators and preaching
friars, clash in my mind — it would be that I might afterward spend an hour
in solitude where the pyramid of Cestius stands against the wall, and points
to the humbler tombs of Keats and Shelley.

Well I remember how you smiled
 To see me write your name upon
The soft sea-sand, "O! what a child!
 You think you're writing upon stone!"
I have since written what no tide
 Shall ever wash away, what men
Unborn shall read o'er ocean wide
 And find Ianthe's name again.

[55]

Love

Ask me no more where Jove bestows,
When June is past, that fading rose;
For in your beauty's orient deep,
These flowers, as in their causes, sleep.

Ask me no more whither do stray
The golden atoms of the day;
For, in pure love, Heaven did prepare
Those powders to enrich your hair.

Ask me no more whither doth haste
The nightingale, when May is past;
For in your sweet dividing throat
She winters, and keeps warm her note.

Ask me no more where those stars light
That downwards fall in dead of night:
For in your eyes they sit, and there
Fixèd become as in their sphere.

Ask me no more if east or west
The phoenix builds her spicy nest:
For unto you at last she flies,
And in your fragrant bosom dies.

William Carew

The light and phantastic summer robe of lust

Jeremy Taylor

Oh, thou art fairer than the evening air
Clad in the beauty of a thousand stars;
Brighter art thou than flaming Jupiter
When he appeared to hapless Semele:
More lovely than the monarch of the sky
In wanton Arethusa's azured arms:
And none but thou shalt be my paramour.

Marlowe

We two, that with so many thousand sighs
Did buy each other, must poorly sell ourselves
With the rude brevity and discharge of one.
Injurious time now, with a robber's haste,
Crams his rich thievery up, he knows not how:
As many farewells as be stars in heaven,
With distinct breath and consign'd kisses to them,
He fumbles up into a loose adieu;
And scants us with a single famish'd kiss,
Distasted with the salt of broken tears.

Shakespeare

Have you seen but a bright lily grow
    Before rude hands have touched it?
Have you marked but the fall of the snow
    Before the soil hath smutched it?
Have you felt the wool of the beaver,
        Or swan's down ever?
Or have smelt o' the bud of the brier,
        Or the nard in the fire?
Or have tasted the bag of the bee?
O so white; O so soft, O so sweet is she!

Ben Jonson

Antoine et Cléopatre

Tous deux ils regardaient, de la haute terrasse,
L'Egypte s'endormir sous un ciel étouffant
Et le Fleuve, à travers le Delta noir qu'il fend,
Vers Bubaste ou Sais rouler son onde grasse.

Et le Romain sentait sous la lourde cuirasse,
Soldat captif berçant le sommeil d'un enfant,
Ployer et défaillir sur son coeur triomphant
Le corps voluptueux que son étreinte embrasse.

Tournant sa tête pâle entre ses cheveux bruns
Vers celui qu'enivraient d'invincibles parfums,
Elle tendit sa bouche et ses prunelles claires;

Et sur elle courbé, l'ardent Imperator
Vit dans ses larges yeux étoilés de points d'or
Toute une mer immense où fuyaient des galères.

Heredia

Mine by the right of the white election!
Mine by the royal seal!
Mine by the sign in the scarlet prison
Bars cannot conceal!

Mine, here in vision and in veto!
Mine, by the grave's repeal
Titled, confirmed, — delirious charter!
Mine, while the ages steal!

Emily Dickinson

[58]

The Conformers

Yes; we'll wed, my little fay,
    And you shall write you mine,
And in a villa chastely gray
    We'll house, and sleep, and dine.
    But those night-screened, divine,
    Stolen trysts of heretofore,
We of choice ecstasies and fine
            Shall know no more.

The formal faced cohue
    Will then no more upbraid
With smiting smiles and whisperings two
    Who have thrown less loves in shade.
    We shall no more evade
    The searching light of sun,
Our game of passion will be played,
            Our dreaming done.

We shall not go in stealth
    To rendezvous unknown,
But friends will ask me of your health,
    And you about my own.
    When we abide alone,
    No leapings each to each,
But syllables in frigid tone
            Of household speech.

When down to dust we glide
    Men will not say askance,
As now: 'How all the country side
    Rings with their mad romance!'
    But as they graveward glance
    Remark: 'In them we lose
A worthy pair, who helped advance
            Sound parish views.'

Hardy

[59]

Arab Love Song

The hunchèd camels of the night[1]
Trouble the bright
And silver waters of the moon.
The Maiden of the Morn will soon
Through Heaven stray and sing,
Star gathering.

Now while the dark about our loves is strewn,
Light of my dark, blood of my heart, O come!
And night will catch her breath up, and be dumb.

Leave thy father, leave thy mother
And thy brother;
Leave the black tents of thy tribe apart!
Am I not thy father and thy brother,
And thy mother?
And thou — what needest with thy tribe's black tents
Who hast the red pavilion of my heart?

Francis Thompson

Wild nights! Wild nights!
Were I with thee,
Wild nights should be
Our luxury!

Futile the winds
To a heart in port, —
Done with the compass,
Done with the chart.

Rowing in Eden!
Ah! The sea!
Might I but moor
Tonight in thee!

Emily Dickinson

[1] The cloud-shapes often observed by travellers in the East.

We saw the swallows gathering in the sky,
And in the osier-isle we heard their noise.
We had not to look back on summer joys,
Or forward to a summer of bright dye:
But in the largeness of the evening earth
Our spirits grew as we went side by side.
The hour became her husband and my bride.
Love that had robbed us so, thus blessed our dearth!
The pilgrims of the year waxed very loud
In multitudinous chatterings, as the flood
Full brown came from the West, and like pale blood
Expanded to the upper crimson cloud.
Love that had robbed us of immortal things,
This little moment mercifully gave
Where I have seen across the twilight wave,
The swan sail with her young beneath her wings.

Meredith

Thus piteously Love closed what he begat:
The union of this ever-diverse pair!
These two were rapid falcons in a snare,
Condemned to do the flitting of the bat.
Lovers beneath the singing sky of May,
They wandered once; clear as the dew on flowers:
But they fed not on the advancing hours:
Their hearts held cravings for the buried day.
Then each applied to each that fatal knife,
Deep questioning, which probes to endless dole.
Ah, what a dusty answer gets the soul
When hot for certainties in this our life! —
In tragic hints here see what evermore
Moves dark as yonder midnight ocean's force,
Thundering like ramping hosts of warrior horse,
To throw that faint thin line upon the shore!

Meredith

So, dearest, now thy brows are cold,
   I see thee what thou art, and know
     Thy likeness to the wise below,
Thy kindred with the great of old.

But there is more that I can see,
   And what I see I leave unsaid,
     Nor speak it, knowing Death has made
His darkness beautiful with thee.

Tennyson

Votre personne, vos moindres mouvements, me semblaient avoir dans le monde une importance extra-humaine. Mon coeur comme de la poussière se soulevait derrière vos pas. Vous me faisiez l'effet d'un clair-de-lune par une nuit d'été, quand tout est parfums, ombres douces, blancheurs, infini; et les délices de la chair et de l'âme étaient contenues pour moi dans votre nom que je me répétais en tachant de le baiser sur mes lèvres. Quelquefois vos paroles me reviennent comme un écho lointain, comme le son d'une cloche apporté par le vent; et il me semble que vous êtes là quand je lis des passages de l'amour dans les livres . . . Tout ce qu'on y blâme d'exagéré, vous me l'avez fait ressentir.

Flaubert

Ache deep; but make no moans:
Smile out; but stilly suffer:
The paths of love are rougher
Than thoroughfares of stones.

Hardy

[62]

Why did you let your eyes so rest on me,
  And hold your breath between?
In all the ages this can never be
  As if it had not been.

Mary Coleridge

A Farewell

With all my will, but much against my heart,
We two now part.
My Very Dear,
Our solace is, the sad road lies so clear.
It needs no art,
With faint, averted feet
And many a tear,
In our opposed paths to persevere.
Go thou to East, I West.
We will not say
There's any hope, it is so far away.
But, O, my Best,
When the one darling of our widowhead,
The nursling Grief,
Is dead,
And no dews blur our eyes
To see the peach-bloom come in evening skies,
Perchance we may,
Where now this night is day,
And even through faith of still averted feet,
Making full circle of our banishment,
Amazed meet;
The bitter journey to the bourne so sweet
Seasoning the termless feast of our content
With tears of recognition never dry.

Coventry Patmore

Memory

One had a lovely face,
And two or three had charm,
But charm and face were in vain
Because the mountain grass
Cannot but keep the form
Where the mountain hare has lain.

Yeats

If you were coming in the fall,
I'd brush the summer by
With half a smile and half a spurn,
As housewives do a fly.

Emily Dickinson

I will not count the years — there are days too —
And to-night again I have said
'What if you should be lying dead?'
Well, if it were so, I could only lay my head
Quietly on the pillow of my bed
Thinking of Him on whom poor sufferers cried
Suffering Himself so much before He died:
And then of Judas walking three years by His side,
How Judas kissed Him — how He was crucified.
Always when I see you
I see those two;
Oh! God it is true
We do not, all of us, know what we do:
But Judas knew.

Charlotte Mew

Hot through Troy's ruin Menelaus broke
   To Priam's palace, sword in hand, to sate
   On that adulterous whore a ten years' hate
And a king's honour. Through red death, and smoke,
And cries, and then by quieter ways he strode,
   Till the still innermost chamber fronted him.
   He swung his sword, and crashed into the dim
Luxurious bower, flaming like a god.

High sat white Helen, lovely and serene.
   He had not remembered that she was so fair,
And that her neck curved down in such a way;
And he felt tired. He flung the sword away,
   And kissed her feet, and knelt before her there,
The perfect Knight before the perfect Queen.

Rupert Brooke

Mortality is but the Stuff you wear
To show the better on the imperfect sight.
Your home is surely with the changeless light
Of which you are the daughter and the heir.
For as you pass, the natural life of things
Proclaims the Resurrection: as you pass
Remembered summer shines across the grass
And somewhat in me of the immortal sings.

You were not made for memory, you are not
Youth's accident I think but heavenly more;
Moulding to meaning slips my pen's poor blot
And opening wide that long forbidden door
   Where stands the Mother of God, your exemplar.
   How beautiful, how beautiful you are!

Belloc

Song (Air 'Dermott')

Love was once light as air
Brushed over all my thoughts and themes:
Love once seemed kind as air
When the dewfall gleams.
Now he's another thing —
Naked light, oh hard to bear,
Too much discovering
With his noonday beams.

Long had I sought for you,
Long, long by subtle masks delayed:
Fair shapes I thought were you
On my green heart played.
Now love at his height informs
All that was so vague to view,
Shall not those slighter forms
In his noon hour fade?

Fade they then fast as snow
When April brings the earth to light,
One shape — alas, 'tis so —
Still lingers white:
One heartwrung phantom still,
One I would not tell to go,
Shadows my noontime still
And haunts my night.

C. Day Lewis

Ton âme est un lac d'amour
Dont mes désirs sont les cygnes.

Armand Renaud

Butterflies are white and blue
In this field we wander through.
Suffer me to take your hand.
Death comes in a day or two.
All the things we ever knew
Will be ashes in that hour,
Mark the transient butterfly,
How he hangs upon the flower.
Suffer me to take your hand.
Suffer me to cherish you
Till the dawn is in the sky.
Whether I be false or true,
Death comes in a day or two.

Edna St Vincent Millay

As I sat at my old desk, writing
in golden evening sunshine,
my wife came in suddenly
and, standing beside me,
said 'I love you'
(this year she will be sixty-three and I shall be sixty-eight).
Then I looked at her and saw
not the grey-haired woman but the girl I married in 1922:
poetry shining through that faithful prose,
a fresh flower in bloom.
I said 'You are a rose'
(Thinking how awful it would have been if I had missed her)
and I kissed her.

V. de Sola Pinto

[67]

Napoleon

Bonaparte had perhaps the fewest virtues, and the faintest semblance of them, of any man who has risen by his own efforts to supreme power: and yet the services he rendered to society, incommensurate as they were with the prodigious means he possessed, were great, manifold, and extensive.

Landor

France he quickly made the first nation in the world, first in all the efficiencies both of war and peace; with only two exceptions, that he left the sea out of his conception of war and liberty out of his conception of peace. In energy of mind and body he has probably never had a superior. And if, as Meredith said, this 'hugest of engines' was 'a much limited man', yet the thunder of the engine shook Europe out of her slumbers as she had not been shaken since she heard the disturbing voice of Luther.

John Bailey

He, did he love her? France was his weapon, shrewd
At edge, a wind in onset: he loved well
His tempered weapon, with the which he hewed
Clean to the ground impediments, or hacked,
Sure of the blade that served the great man-miracle.
He raised her, robed her, gemmed her for his bride,
Did but her blood in blindness given exact.
Her blood she gave, was blind to him as guide:
She quivered at his word, and at his touch
Was hound or steed for any mark he espied,
He loved her more than little, less than much.

Meredith

[68]

Il pensait ce que pensait tout grenadier de son armée; mais il le pensait avec une force inouïe.

Anatole France

I used to say of him that his presence on the field made the difference of forty thousand men.

Wellington

Demain, c'est le cheval qui s'abat blanc d'écume.
Demain, o conquérant, c'est Moscou qui s'allume,
    La nuit, comme un flambeau.
C'est votre vieille garde au loin jonchant la plaine,
Demain, c'est Waterloo! Demain, c'est Sainte-Hélène!
    Demain, c'est le tombeau!

Victor Hugo

After Waterloo

Spirit Ironic

Nothing care I for these high-doctrined dreams,
And shape the case in quite a common way,
So I would ask, Ajaccian Bonaparte,
Has all this been worth while?

Napoléon

    O cursèd hour,
Why am I stung by spectral questionings?
Did not my clouded soul incline to match
Those of the corpses yonder, thou should'st rue
Thy saying, Fiend, whoever thou may'st be! . . .
    Why did the death-drops fail to bite me close

[69]

I took at Fontainebleau? Had I then ceased,
This deep had been unplumbed; had they but worked,
I had thrown three-fold the glow of Hannibal
Down History's dusky lanes! — Is it too late? . . .
Yea. Self-sought death would smoke but damply here!
    If but a Kremlin cannon-shot had met me
My greatness would have stood: I should have scored
A vast repute, scarce paralleled in time.
As it did not, the fates had served me best
If in the thick and thunder of to-day,
Like Nelson, Harold, Hector, Cyrus, Saul,
I had been shifted from this jail of flesh,
To wander as a greatened ghost elsewhere.
— Yes, a good death, to have died on yonder field;
But never a ball came passing down my way!
    So, as it is, a miss-mark they will dub me;
And yet — I found the crown of France in the mire,
And with the point of my prevailing sword
I picked it up! But for all this and this
I shall be nothing . . .
To shoulder Christ from out the topmost niche
In human fame, as once I fondly felt,
Was not for me. I came too late in time
To assume the prophet or the demi-god,
A part past playing now. My only course
To make good showance to posterity
Was to implant my line upon the throne.
And how shape that, if now extinction nears?
Great men are meteors that consume themselves
To light the earth. This is my burnt-out hour.

Hardy

A St Helena Lullaby

'How far is St Helena from a little child at play?'
What makes you want to wander there with all the world between?
Oh, Mother, call your son again or else he'll run away.
(*No one thinks of winter when the grass is green!*)

'How far is St Helena from a fight in Paris street?'
I haven't time to answer now — the men are falling fast.
The guns begin to thunder, and the drums begin to beat.
(*If you take the first step, you will take the last!*)

'How far is St Helena from the field of Austerlitz?'
You couldn't hear me if I told — so loud the cannon roar.
But not so far for people who are living by their wits.
(*'Gay go up' means 'Gay go down' the wide world o'er!*)

'How far is St Helena from an Emperor of France?'
I cannot see — I cannot tell — the crowns they dazzle so.
The Kings sit down to dinner, and the Queens stand up to dance.
(*After open weather you may look for snow!*)

'How far is St Helena from the Capes of Trafalgar?'
A longish way — a longish way — with ten year more to run.
It's South across the water underneath a falling star.
(*What you cannot finish you must leave undone!*)

'How far is St Helena from the Beresina ice?'
An ill way — a chill way — the ice begins to crack.
But not so far for gentlemen who never took advice.
(*When you can't go forward you must e'en come back!*)

'How far is St Helena from the field of Waterloo?'
A near way — a clear way — the ship will take you soon.
A pleasant place for gentlemen with little left to do.
(*Morning never tries you till the afternoon!*)

'How far from St Helena to the Gate of Heaven's Grace?'
That no one knows — that no one knows — and no one ever will.
But fold your hands across your heart and cover up your face,
And after all your trapesings, child, lie still!

Kipling

Places

[The Monster London]

Whilst this hard truth I teach, methinks I see
The Monster London laugh at me.
I should at thee too, foolish city,
if it were fit to laugh at misery,
But thy estate I pity.

Let but thy wicked men from out thee go,
And all the fools that crowd thee so;
even thou, who dost thy millions boast,
a village less than Islington wilt grow,
a solitude almost.

Cowley

[Swaledale]

'And he had trudged through Yorkshire dales,
Among the rocks and winding *scars*;
Where deep and low the hamlets lie
Beneath their little patch of sky
And little lot of stars . . .'

The Swale flowed under the grey rocks,
But he flowed quiet and unseen:—
You need a strong and stormy gale
To bring the noises of the Swale
To that green spot, so calm and green!

Wordsworth

[A London Particular]

Fog everywhere. Fog up the river, where it flows among green aits and meadows; fog down the river, where it rolls defiled among the tiers of shipping, and the waterside pollutions of a great (and dirty) city. Fog on the Essex marshes, fog on the Kentish heights. Fog creeping into the cabooses of collier-brigs; fog lying out on the yards, and hovering in the rigging of great ships; fog drooping on the gunwales of barges and small boats. Fog in the eyes and throats of ancient Greenwich pensioners, wheezing by the firesides of their wards; fog in the stem and bowl of the afternoon pipe of the wrathful skipper, down in his close cabin; fog cruelly pinching the toes and fingers of his shivering little 'prentice boy on deck. Chance people on the bridges peeping over the parapets into a nether sky of fog, with fog all round them, as if they were up in a balloon, and hanging in the misty clouds.

Gas looming through the fog in divers places in the streets, much as the sun may, from the spongey fields, be seen to loom by husbandman and ploughboy. Most of the shops lighted two hours before their time — as the gas seems to know, for it has a haggard and unwilling look.

The raw afternoon is rawest, and the dense fog is densest, and the muddy streets are muddiest, near that leaden-headed old obstruction, appropriate ornament for the threshold of a leaden-headed old corporation: Temple Bar. And hard by Temple Bar, in Lincoln's Inn Hall, at the very heart of the fog, sits the Lord High Chancellor in his High Court of Chancery.

Never can there come fog too thick, never can there come mud and mire too deep, to assort with the groping and floundering condition which this High Court of Chancery, most pestilent of hoary sinners, holds, this day, in the sight of heaven and earth.

Dickens

[Bly]

But there was everything, for our apprehension, in the lucky fact that no discomfortable legend, no perturbation of scullions, had ever, within any-one's memory, attached to the kind old place.

Henry James

[73]

Almae Matres

(St Andrews, 1862.   Oxford, 1865)

St Andrews by the northern sea,
   A haunted town it is to me!
A little city, worn and gray,
   The gray North Ocean girds it round;
And o'er the rocks, and up the bay,
   The long sea-rollers surge and sound;
And still the thin and biting spray
   Drives down the melancholy street,
And still endure, and still decay,
   Towers that the salt winds vainly beat.
Ghost-like and shadowy they stand
   Dim mirrored in the wet sea-sand.

O ruined chapel! long ago
   We loitered idly where the tall
Fresh budded mountain ashes blow
   Within thy desecrated wall:
The tough roots rent the tomb below,
   The April birds sang clamorous,
We did not dream, we could not know,
   How hardly fate would deal with us!

O broken minster, looking forth
   Beyond the bay, above the town!
O winter of the kindly north,
   O college of the scarlet gown,
And shining sands beside the sea,
   And stretch of links beyond the sand,
Once more I watch you, and to me
   It is as if I touched his hand!

And therefore art thou yet more dear,
   O little city, gray and sere,
Though shrunken from thine ancient pride
   And lonely by thy lonely sea,
Than these fair halls on Isis' side,
   Where youth an hour came back to me!

A land of waters green and clear,
  Of willows and of poplars tall,
And, in the spring-time of the year,
  The white may breaking over all,
And Pleasure quick to come at call.

  And summer rides by marsh and wold,
  And autumn with her crimson pall
    About the towers of Magdalen rolled;
  And strange enchantments from the past,
    And memories of the friends of old,
  And strong Tradition, binding fast
    The 'flying terms' with bands of gold, —

All these hath Oxford: all are dear,
  But dearer far the little town,
The drifting surf, the wintry year,
  The college of the scarlet gown,
    St Andrews by the northern sea,
    That is a haunted town to me!

                              Andrew Lang

[The Sense of England]

But there was another admonition that was almost equally sure to descend
upon his spirit in a summer hour, in a stroll about the grand abbey; to sink
into it as the light lingered on the rough red walls and the local accent of the
children sounded soft in the churchyard. It was simply the sense of England
— a sort of apprehended revelation of this country. The dim annals of the
place appeared to be in the air (foundations bafflingly early, a great monastic
life, wars of the Roses, with battles and blood in the streets, and then the long
quietude of the respectable centuries, all corn-fields and magistrates and
vicars), and these things were connected with an emotion that arose from the
green country, the rich land so infinitely lived in, and laid on him a hand that
was too ghostly to press and yet somehow too urgent to be light. It produced
a throb that he could not have spoken of, it was so deep, and that was half
imagination and half responsibility.

                                              Henry James

[Scotland]

In the highlands, in the country places,
Where the old plain men have rosy faces,
And the young fair maidens
Quiet eyes;
Where essential silence cheers and blesses,
And for ever in the hill-recesses
Her more lovely music
Broods and dies.

O to mount again where erst I haunted;
Where the old red hills are bird-enchanted,
And the low green meadows
Bright with sward;
And when even dies, the million-tinted,
And the night has come, and planets glinted,
Lo, the valley hollow
Lamp-bestarred!

O to dream, O to awake and wander
There, and with delight to take and render,
Through the trance of silence,
Quiet breath;
Lo! for there, among the flowers and grasses,
Only the mightier movement sounds and passes;
Only winds and rivers,
Life and death.

Stevenson

[Stonehenge]

What is Stonehenge? It is the roofless past;
Man's ruinous myth; his uninterred adoring
Of the unknown in sunrise cold and red;
His quest of stars that arch his doomed exploring.

And what it Time but shadows that were cast
By these storm-sculptured stones while centuries fled?

The stones remain; their stillness can outlast
The skies of history hurrying overhead.

Sassoon

[76]

Wiltshire Downs

The cuckoo's double note
Loosened like bubbles from a drowning throat
Floats through the air
In mockery of pipit, lark and stare.

The stable-boys thud by
Their horses slinging divots at the sky
And with bright hooves
Printing the sodden turf with lucky grooves.

As still as a windhover
A shepherd in his flapping coat leans over
His tall sheep-crook
And shearlings, tegs and yoes cons like a book.

And one tree-crowned long barrow
Stretched like a sow that has brought forth her farrow
Hides a king's bones
Lying like broken sticks among the stones.

Andrew Young

Ancestors

I have forgotten the country in the North, where my people
  lived before me.
The stone walls curving over green hills; the air as pure as spirits
  could breathe in heaven, but much more cold.
The cry of the curlews, like a voice given to the sky; the dark
  bogs and the stones.
The brown streams, always talking to the lonely sheep.
My people before me had brown eyes like the streams, and bodies
  built to endure the battering wind like walls. And their forgotten faces, I think, were shy, resolved, and fresh.
They lived in stone houses, under the black-shadowing syca-
  mores.
They knew the rent sky sweeping over the moors on stormy
  days, like passion in unspeaking hearts.
And I, in this protected house, breathing the hot air, I have forgotten that my people came from the North.

Frances Cornford

[Lord's Cricket Ground]

All is in all, the wise men say, for to know and believe this is to be invulnerable, incapable of loss; but we are men and women, deeply vulnerable still as children are, and when the cupboard is to be open for only a few hours it is the devil to choose among our toys. In any case, so many of the toys we want are put away on the topmost shelf until the Germans are tired of their game, and perversely we long for them. For example, to be at Lord's for there nothing changes. A new stand or a new scoring-board arises now and then, bowlers cease to bowl trial balls, red bat-handles go out of fashion, but there is always the same freshness in the forenoon, the same air of hot endurance between luncheon and tea, and, after tea, the same intensification of sound and silence, the lengthening of shadows, the deepening of the green, and, it may be, suddenly an unreal tension exquisitely heightened so that each withdrawal to the pavilion is the death of a warrior and each new entrant a David come to battle. And when it is over and you are calling a hansom, what will the newsboy slip from under his arm — a green *Westminster* or a pink *Globe*? And at what time will the curtain rise on Lehar at Daly's?

The nostalgia for cricket seems a kind of madness to those who have it not. They come late in life or from foreign parts willing to be instructed in the mysteries and, being instructed, are still inexpressibly bored; they cannot understand what we see in the game. The answer is that it is not the game only that we see, but childhood and youth, and peace of mind in the recollection of enduring things:

> For the field is full of shades as I near the shadowy coast,
> And a ghostly batsman plays to the bowling of a ghost,
> And I look through my tears on a soundless-clapping host
> As the run-stealers flicker to and fro,
> To and fro:—
> O my Hornby and my Barlow long ago!

A day at Lord's, with past welling up into the present, puts a bracket round controversy and gives imagination release. There are two minds — the mind that keeps its eye on the ball, and the mind that ranges. 'So then the princess threw the ball at one of her company; she missed the girl, and cast the ball into the deep . . .' Whereupon, it will be remembered, all of them, being women, raised a piercing cry, and the goodly Odysseus awoke and sat up, and observed that another wicket had fallen, Trumper was out, and the Eighth Army had advanced on Carthage.

Charles Morgan (written in 1943)

[78]

Adlestrop

Yes. I remember Adlestrop —
The name, because one afternoon
Of heat the express-train drew up there
Unwontedly. It was late June.

The steam hissed. Someone cleared his throat.
No one left and no one came
On the bare platform. What I saw
Was Adlestrop — only the name

And willows, willow-herb, and grass,
And meadowsweet, and haycocks dry,
No whit less still and lonely fair
Than the high cloudlets in the sky.

And for that minute a blackbird sang
Close by, and round him, mistier,
Farther and farther, all the birds
Of Oxfordshire and Gloucestershire.

Edward Thomas

[Foston]

My living in Yorkshire was so far out of the way that it was actually twelve
miles from a lemon.

Sydney Smith

[Rivers]

For they are new, they are fresh; there's no surprise
    Like theirs on earth. O strange for evermore!
This moment's Tiber with his shining eyes
    Never saw Rome before.

Alice Meynell

[79]

To Eton: Fifty Years After

You run in my heart like a tune in the head;
  Uninvited, at ease,
You bring elms and red bricks to my walks or my bed,
  — Small bricks and great trees.

From Keate's Lane in half-shadow I see brightness fall
  Through a tree-top, to dapple
Finch-Hatton's lithe form as he droops on the Wall,
  With his back to the Chapel.

You come of a sudden to set me afloat
  In a water-borne dream,
Where I skirt Upper Hope with my chair for a boat
  On a wavering stream.

When gusty November has blown the leaf-scud
  To ruinous rout,
And stays to draw breath, I can hear the thud, thud
  Of a School Kickabout.

A whiff from the tarmac is potent to call
  Me away from this street
To a fives-court in March, and the click of the ball,
  And the padding of feet.

If some pinnacled Abbey stands up on the plain
  With small tenements round her,
I recall the loose rally of roofs to the Fane
  Of Henry our Founder.

You come at odd times, as a caller unknown,
  To entangle and hold me;
You make me Curator of things you have shown,
  Of things you have told, me.

Where turf is sun-warmed, if elm-shadows are long,
  When a river is cool,
You come haunting my head and my heart like a song,
  — And men call you a School!

L. E. Jones

[80]

Poetry

Poetry is the honey of all flowers, the quintessence of all sciences, the marrow of wit and the very phrase of angels.

Thomas Nashe

Every true lover of poetry knows that when he cites great lines it is not the poetry but the hearer that is to be judged.

Coventry Patmore

On ne peut trouver de poésie nulle part quand on n'en porte en soi.

Joubert

All that is worth remembering of life is the poetry of it.

Hazlitt

No blazoned banner we unfold —
One charge alone we give to youth,
Against the sceptred myth to hold
The golden heresy of truth.

A. E. (George Russell)

Slow, slow, fresh fount, keep time with my salt tears;
Yet slower, yet; O faintly, gentle springs;
List to the heavy part the music bears,
   Woe weeps out her division when she sings.
     Droop herbs and flowers;
     Fall grief in showers;
     Our beauties are not ours;
       O, I could still,
Like melting snow upon some craggy hill,
     Drop, drop, drop, drop,
Since Nature's pride is now a withered daffodil.

Ben Jonson

Mock on, Mock on, Voltaire, Rousseau:
Mock on, Mock on: 'tis all in vain!
You throw the sand against the wind,
And the wind blows it back again.

And every sand becomes a Gem
Reflected in the beams divine;
Blown back they blind the mocking Eye,
But still in Israel's paths they shine.

The Atoms of Democritus
And Newton's Particles of light
Are sands upon the Red sea shore,
Where Israel's tents do shine so bright.

Blake

Not knowing when the dawn will come
I open every door.
Or has it feathers like a bird,
Or billows like a shore?

Emily Dickinson

The lowest trees have tops, the ant her gall,
    The fly her spleen, the little sparks their heat;
The slender hairs cast shadows, though but small,
    And bees have stings, although they be not great;
Seas have their source, and so have shallow springs;
And love is love, in beggars as in kings.

Where rivers smoothest run, deep are the fords;
    The dial stirs, yet none perceives it move;
The firmest faith is in the fewest words;
    The turtles cannot sing, and yet they love:
True hearts have eyes and ears, no tongues to speak;
They hear and see, and sigh, and then they break.

Sir Edward Dyer

On a poet's lips I slept
Dreaming like a love-adept
In the sound his breathing kept;
Nor seeks nor finds he mortal blisses,
But feeds on the aëreal kisses
Of shapes that haunt thought's wildernesses.
He will watch from dawn to gloom
The lake-reflected sun illume
The yellow bees in the ivy-bloom,
Nor heed nor see, what things they be;
But from these create he can
Forms more real than living man,
Nurslings of immortality!
One of these awakened me,
And I sped to succour thee.

Shelley

The pedigree of honey
Does not concern the bee;
A clover, any time, to him
Is aristocracy.

Emily Dickinson

[83]

A Song of Derivations

I come from nothing; but from where
Come the undying thoughts I bear?
   Down, through long links of death and birth,
   From the past poets of the earth.
My Immortality is there.

I am like the blossom of an hour.
But long, long vanished sun and shower
   Awoke my breath i' the young world's air.
   I track the past back everywhere
Through seed and flower and seed and flower.

Or I am like a stream that flows
Full of the cold springs that arose
   In morning lands, in distant hills;
   And down the plain my channel fills
With melting of forgotten snows.

Voices, I have not heard, possessed
My own fresh songs; my thoughts are blessed
   With relics of the far unknown.
   And mixed with memories not my own
The sweet streams throng into my breast.

Before this life began to be,
The happy songs that wake in me
   Woke long ago and far apart.
   Heavily on this little heart
Presses this immortality.

Alice Meynell

The Dream

I slept and thought a letter came from you —
You did not love me any more, it said.
What breathless grief! my love not true, not true . . .
I was afraid of people, and afraid
Of everything — of the cold wind that blew,

The clock, the wooden chair; and so I strayed
From home, but could not stray from fear, I knew.
And then at dawn I woke and wept and prayed,
And knew my blesséd love was still the same; —
And yet I sit and moan upon the bed
For that dream-creature's grief. For when I came
(I came perhaps to comfort her) she fled.
I would be with her where she wanders now,
Fleeing the earth with pain upon her brow.

Viola Meynell

My former thoughts returned: the fear that kills;
And hope that is unwilling to be fed;
Cold, pain, and labour, and all fleshly ills;
And mighty Poets in their misery dead.

Wordsworth

The Merciful Knight

Swift, in a moment's thought, our lastingness is wrought
From life, the transient wing.
Swift, in a moment's light, he mercy found, that knight
Who rode alone in spring . . .
The knight who sleeps in stone with ivy overgrown
Knew this miraculous thing.
In a moment of the years the sun, like love through tears,
Shone where the rain went by.
In a world where armoured men made swords their strength and then
Rode darkly out to die,
One heart was there estranged; one heart, one heart was changed
While the cloud crossed the sun . . .
Mercy from long ago, be mine that I may know
Life's lastingness begun.

Sassoon

To suffer woes which Hope thinks infinite;
To forgive wrongs darker than death or night;
   To defy Power, which seems omnipotent;
To love, and bear; to hope till Hope creates
From its own wreck the thing it contemplates;
   Neither to change, nor falter, nor repent;
This, like thy glory, Titan, is to be
Good, great and joyous, beautiful and free;
This is alone Life, Joy, Empire, and Victory.

Shelley

Time and Twilight

In the dark twilight of an autumn morn,
I stood within a little country-town,
Wherefrom a long acquainted path went down
To the dear village haunts where I was born;
The low of oxen on the rainy wind,
Death and the Past, came up the well-known road,
And bathed my heart with tears, but stirr'd my mind
To tread once more the track so long untrod;
But I was warn'd, 'Regrets which are not thrust
Upon thee, seek not; for this sobbing breeze
Will but unman thee; thou art bold to trust
Thy woe-worn thoughts among these roaring trees,
And gleams of by-gone playgrounds — Is't no crime
To rush by night into the arms of Time?'

Charles Tennyson Turner

I cannot pray with my head
Nor aspire from bended knees;
But I saw in a dream the dead
Moving among green trees.

I saw the living green
Uprising from the rock.
This have I surely seen,
Though the morning mind may mock.

Sassoon

Values

Till darkness lays a hand on these gray eyes
And out of man my ghost is sent alone,
It is my chance to know that force and size
Are nothing but by answered undertone.
No beauty even of absolute perfection
Dominates here — the glance, the pause, the guess
Must be my amulets of resurrection;
Raindrops may murder, lightnings may caress.

There I was tortured, but I cannot grieve;
There crowned and palaced — visibles deceive.
That storm of belfried cities in my mind
Leaves me my vespers cool and eglantined.
From love's wide-flowering mountain-side I chose
This sprig of green, in which an angel shows.

Blunden

I look into my glass,
And view my wasting skin,
And say, 'Would God it came to pass
My heart had shrunk as thin!'

For then, I, undistrest
By hearts grown cold to me,
Could lonely wait my endless rest
With equanimity.

But Time, to make me grieve,
Part steals, lets part abide;
And shakes this fragile frame at eve
With throbbings of noontide.

Hardy

Egypt's might is tumbled down
   Down a-Down the deeps of thought;
Greece is fallen and Troy town;
Glorious Rome hath lost her crown,
   Venice' pride is nought.

But the dreams their children dreamed,
   Fleeting, unsubstantial, vain,
Shadowy as the shadows seemed,
Airy nothing, as they deemed,
   These remain.

Mary Coleridge

Log Fire

The homely fire dies down.
Slowly the embers fade
Into the tomb of ash
The flames have made.
Proud trees from forests felled
That gave us shade and heat
Come in the end to this
Dust at our feet.
But we of greater pride,
The anxious, fearful we,
In colder dust subside
Within a tree.

Harry Conway

Innocent's Song

Who's that knocking on the window,
Who's that standing at the door,
What are all those presents
Lying on the kitchen floor?

Who is the smiling stranger
With hair as white as gin,
What is he doing with the children
And who could have let him in?

Why has he rubies on his fingers,
A cold, cold crown on his head,
Why, when he caws his carol,
Does the salty snow run red?

Why does he ferry my fireside
As a spider on a thread,
His fingers made of fuses
And his tongue of gingerbread?

Why does the world before him
Melt in a million suns,
Why do his yellow-yearning eyes
Burn like saffron buns?

Watch where he comes walking
Out of the Christmas flame,
Dancing, double-talking:

Herod is his name.

Charles Causley

Words

Out of us all
That make rhymes,
Will you choose
Sometimes —
As the winds use
A crack in a wall
Or a drain,
Their joy or their pain
To whistle through —
Choose me,
You English words?

I know you:
You are light as dreams,
Tough as oak,
Precious as gold,
As poppies and corn,
Or an old cloak:
Sweet as our birds
To the ear,
As the burnet rose
In the heat
Of Midsummer:
Strange as the races
Of dead and unborn:
Strange and sweet
Equally,
And familiar,
To the eye,
As the dearest faces
That a man knows,
And as lost homes are:
But though older far
Than oldest yew, —
As our hills are, old, —
Worn new
Again and again:

Young as our streams
After rain:
And as dear
As the earth which you prove
That we love.

Make me content
With some sweetness
From Wales
Whose nightingales
Have no wings, —
From Wiltshire and Kent
And Herefordshire,
And the villages there, —
From the names, and the things
No less.

Let me sometimes dance
With you,
Or climb
Or stand perchance
In ecstasy,
Fixed and free
In a rhyme,
As poets do.

Edward Thomas

To Pauline, with a looking-glass

A lovely portrait, all admit,
   Is of a lovely frame deserving,
And what for masterpiece more fit
   Than elegance of gilded curving?

Yet how inadequate, how tame,
   This gold, these curves will seem, alas,
Compared with what they'll have to frame
   Whenever you take up this glass.

Martyn Skinner

Readers and Writers

It is a terrible alternative that an author must either starve and be esteemed, or be vilified and get money.

Fanny Burney

Il me semble qu'il faut du courage à l'écrivain presque autant qu'au guerrier; l'un ne doit plus songer aux journalistes que l'autre à l'hôpital.

Stendhal

It is dangerous to have any intercourse or dealing with small authors. They are as troublesome to handle, as easy to discompose, as difficult to pacify, and leave as unpleasant marks on you, as children.

Landor

The poor people seem to think a style can be put off or put on, not like a skin but like a coat. Is not a skin verily a product and close kinsfellow of all that lies under it, exact type of the nature of the beast, not to be plucked off without flaying and death? The Public is an old woman, let her maunder and mumble.

Carlyle

I begin to perceive that if a man will be an author, he must live neither to himself nor to his friends, so much as to others, whom he never saw nor shall see.

Cowper

The only indisputable proof of an author possessing style is his being unquotable except in his own words. If a paraphrase will do he may have learning, wisdom, profundity, what you will, but style he has not. Style is the expression of an individual, appearing once and only once in the world; it is Keats or Carlyle or Swinburne: it never has been and never will be anybody else.

John Bailey

The man who has no feeling for old books because they are old lacks something of literature. Everything that is old yet still lives has a title to reverence, for it has been spared by Time the winnower, whose forbearance is a patent of nobility. But an old book has more than the dignity of age; it has a piece of immortality as well. Since a book is not a disembodied spirit, but soul compact with clay, the gayest and most prosperous of new editions may suggest to a sensitive imagination an incongruity as of varnished decay, a hint of grave-clothes beneath the trappings. But the grace of an old book is vernal and autumnal. It is as old as the date on its title-page, and as young as the hour it was born. It has distilled from the homage of generations the incense it could draw, and has kept all the freshness of a budding flower.

R. W. Chapman

The world of books is the most remarkable creation of man. Nothing else that he builds ever lasts. Nations perish. Civilisations grow old and die out, and after an era of darkness new races build others, but in the world of books are volumes that have seen this happen again and again and yet live on, still young, still as fresh as the day they were written, still telling men's hearts of the hearts of men centuries dead.

Clarence Day

[93]

Consolation

The other day, depressed on the Underground, I tried to cheer myself by thinking over the joys of our human lot. But there wasn't one of them for which I seemed to care a button — not Wine, nor Friendship, nor Eating, nor Making Love, nor the Consciousness of Virtue. Was it worth while then going up in a lift into a world that had nothing less trite to offer?

Then I thought of reading — the nice and subtle happiness of reading. This was enough, this joy not dulled by Age, this polite and unpunished vice, this selfish, serene, life-long intoxication.[1]

Logan Pearsall Smith

Never ask anybody, if you mean to write anything.

Goethe

The use of much material lifted from the work of one author is to be condemned as plagiarism, whereas the use of much material from the work of many authors is to be praised as research.

Vernon Bartlett

Swift ridiculed the music of Handel and the generalship of Marlborough, Pope the style of Middleton and the scholarship of Bentley, Gray the abilities of Shaftesbury and the eloquence of Rousseau. Shakespeare hardly found those who would collect his tragedies; Milton was read from godliness; Virgil was antiquated and rustic, Cicero Asiatic. What a rabble has persecuted my friend, in these latter times the glory of our country. An elephant is born to be consumed by ants in the midst of his unapproachable solitudes. Wordsworth is the prey of Jeffrey. Why repine? Let us rather amuse ourselves with allegories, and recollect that God in the creation left his noblest creature at the mercy of a serpent.

Landor

[1] From this Valery Larbaud took the title of his book *Ce Vice Impuni, la Lecture* (1936).

But the taste and ideas of one generation are not those of the next. The next generation in its turn arrives; — first its sharp-shooters, its quick-witted, audacious light troops; then the elephantine main body. The imposing array of its predecessors it confidently assails, riddles it with bullets, passes over its body. It goes hard then with many once popular reputations, with many authorities once oracular. Only two kinds of authors are safe in the general havoc. The first kind are the great abounding fountains of truth, whose criticism of life is a source of illumination and joy to the whole human race for ever, — the Homers, the Shakespeares. These are the sacred personages, whom all civilised warfare respects. The second are those whom the out-skirmishers of the new generation, its forerunners, — quick-witted soldiers, as I have said, the select of the army, — recognise, though the bulk of their comrades behind might not, as of the same family and character with the sacred personages, exercising like them an immortal function, and like them inspiring a permanent interest. They snatch them up, and set them in a place of shelter, where the on-coming multitude may not overwhelm them.

Matthew Arnold

Shall These Bones Live?

If all the clocks rang their last chime,
And all the clock-towers toppled, and time
Ran down today,
Chaucer and Blake's haphazard bones
Would not lift their Abbey stones;
And stalk away
Arm in arm, to see the sun
Burn out, or the moon's skeleton
Wasting and frail as they.

Dying, they put the body down
Once and for all like an old gown
In its wooden room.
Each has climbed to a worthier nook
Between the white walls of a book
Till the knock of doom.
This secret every poet knows:
His nib must cut with chisel-blows
The lettering of his tomb.

Jon Stallworthy

[95]

Scott

Scott, the superlative of my comparative.

Byron

When I am very ill indeed, I can read Scott's novels, and they are almost the only books I can then *read.* I cannot at such times read the Bible; my mind reflects on it, but I can't bear the open page.

Coleridge

Now I selected Scott (as a man of energy or genius) for the very reason, that I do hold him for a man of *very extraordinary* powers; and when I say that I have read the far greater part of his novels twice, and several three times over, with undiminished pleasure and interest: and that, in my reprobation of the *Bride of Lammermoor* (with the exception, however of the almost Shakespearian old witch-wives at the funeral) and of the *Ivanhoe*, I mean to imply the grounds of my admiration of the others, and the permanent nature of the interest which they excite. In a word, I am far from thinking that *Old Mortality* or *Guy Mannering* would have been less admired in the age of Sterne, Fielding, and Richardson, than they are in the present times.

Coleridge

I cannot pull well in long traces, in which the draught is too far behind me. I love to have the press thumping, clattering, and banging in my rear; it creates the necessity which almost always makes me work best.

Walter Scott's Journal

'There is one thing I believe peculiar to me — I work, that is, meditate for the purpose of working, best, when I have a *quasi* engagement with some other book for example. When I find myself doing ill, or like to come to a still stand in writing, I take up some slight book, a novel or the like, and usually have not read far ere my difficulties are removed, and I am ready to write again. There must be two currents of ideas going on in my mind at the same time, or perhaps the slighter occupation serves like a woman's wheel or stocking to ballast the mind, as it were, by preventing the thoughts from wandering, and so gives the deeper current the power to flow undisturbed. I always laugh when I hear people say, Do one thing at once. I have done a dozen things at once all my life.'

Journal

'Patience, cousin, and shuffle the cards.'[1]

I am getting very unlocomotive — something like an old cabinet that looks well enough in its own corner, but will scarce bear wheeling about, even to be dusted.

Journal

And so the curtain falls; and the strong Walter Scott is with us no more. A possession from him does remain; widely scattered; yet attainable; not inconsiderable. It can be said of him, When he departed, he took a Man's life along with him. No sounder piece of British manhood was put together in that eighteenth century of Time. Alas, his fine Scotch face, with its shaggy honesty, sagacity and goodness, when we saw it latterly on the Edinburgh streets, was all worn with care, the joy all fled from it; — ploughed deep with labour and sorrow. We shall never forget it; we shall never see it again. Adieu, Sir Walter, pride of all Scotchmen, take our proud and sad farewell.

Carlyle

[1] Scott quoted these words from *Don Quixote* in his journal on hearing the first intimations of his financial ruin.

Spring

O thou with dewy locks, who lookest down
Through the clear windows of the morning, turn
Thine angel eyes upon our western isle,
Which in full choir hails thy approach, O Spring!

The hills tell one another, and the listening
Valleys hear; all our longing eyes are turn'd
Up to thy bright pavilions: issue forth
And let thy holy feet visit our clime!

Come o'er the eastern hills, and let our winds
Kiss thy perfumed garments; let us taste
Thy morn and evening breath; scatter thy pearls
Upon our lovesick land that mourns for thee.

O deck her forth with thy fair fingers; pour
Thy soft kisses on her bosom; and put
Thy golden crown upon her languish'd head,
Whose modest tresses are bound up for thee.

Blake

But where a passion yet unborn perhaps
Lay hidden as the music of the moon
Sleeps in the plain eggs of the nightingale.

Tennyson

The Year's Awakening

How do you know that the pilgrim track
Along the belting zodiac
Swept by the sun in his seeming rounds
Is traced by now to the Fishes' bounds
And into the Ram, when weeks of cloud
Have wrapt the sky in a clammy shroud,
And never as yet a tinct of spring
Has shown in the Earth's apparelling;
   O vespering bird, how do you know,
    How do you know?

How do you know, deep underground,
Hid in your bed from sight and sound,
Without a turn in temperature,
With weather life can scarce endure,
That light has won a fraction's strength,
And day put on some moments' length,
Whereof in merest rote will come,
Weeks hence, mild airs that do not numb,
   O crocus root, how do you know,
    How do you know?

Hardy

For winter's rains and ruins are over,
   And all the season of snows and sins;
The days dividing lover and lover,
   The light that loses, the night that wins;
And time remembered is grief forgotten,
And frosts are slain and flowers begotten,
And in green underwood and cover
   Blossom by blossom the spring begins.

Swinburne

Spring

Nothing is so beautiful as spring —
   When weeds, in wheels, shoot long and lovely and lush;
   Thrush's eggs look little low heavens, and thrush
Through the echoing timber does so rinse and wring
The ear, it strikes like lightnings to hear him sing;
   The glassy peartree leaves and blooms, they brush
   The descending blue; that blue is all in a rush
With richness; the racing lambs too have fair their fling.

What is all this juice and all this joy?
   A strain of the earth's sweet being in the beginning
In Eden garden. — Have, get, before it cloy,
   Before it cloud, Christ, lord, and sour with sinning,
Innocent mind and Mayday in girl and boy,
   Most, O maid's child, thy choice and worthy the winning.

Hopkins

I so liked Spring last year
Because you were here; —
The thrushes too —
Because it was these you so liked to hear.
I so liked you.

This year's a different thing, —
I'll not think of you.
But I'll like spring because it is simply spring
As the thrushes do.

Charlotte Mew

Nothing is certain, only the certain spring.

Laurence Binyon

[100]

Tributes

Near this place lies
CHARLES CLAUDIUS PHILLIPS
whose absolute contempt of riches
and inimitable performances upon the violin
made him the admiration of all that knew him.
He was born in Wales,
made the tour of Europe,
and, after the experience of both kinds of fortune,
Died in 1732.

*Epitaph in the porch of
St Peter's Church, Wolverhampton.*

'The Guards are superior to the Line — not as being picked men like the French — for Napoleon gave peculiar privileges to his guardsmen and governed the army with them — but from the goodness of the non-commissioned officers. They do in fact all that the commissioned officers in the Line are expected to do — and don't do. This must be as long as the present system lasts — and I am all for it — of having gentlemen for officers; you cannot require them to do many things that should be done. They must not speak to the men for instance — we should reprimand them if they did; our system in that respect is so very different from the French. Now all that work is done by the non-commissioned officers of the Guards. It is true that they regularly get drunk once a day — by eight in the evening, and go to bed soon after, but then they always took care to do first whatever they were bid. When I had given an officer in the Guards an order, I felt sure of its being executed; but with an officer in the Line, it was, I will venture to say, a hundred to one against its being done at all.'

Wellington

Never until now, most holy father, did I hope or desire to offer my homage to any potentate on earth; and now I offer it only to the highest of them all.

There was a time when the cultivators of literature were permitted and expected to bring the fruit of their labour to the Vatican. Not only was incense welcome there, but even the humblest produce of the poorest soil.

Verbenas, pueri, ponite turaque.[1]

If those better days are returning, without what was bad or exceptionable in them, the glory is due entirely to your Holiness. You have restored to Italy hope and happiness; to the rest of the world hope only. But a single word from your prophetic lips, a single motion of your earth-embracing arm, will overturn the firmest seats of iniquity and oppression. The word must be spoken; the arm must wave. What do we see before us? If we take the best of rulers under our survey, we find selfishness and frivolity: if we extend the view, ingratitude, disregard of honour, contempt of honesty, breach of promises: one step yet beyond, and there is cold-blooded idiocy, stabbing the nobles at home, spurning the people everywhere, and voiding its corrosive slaver in the fair face of Italy. It is better to look no further, else our eyes must be riveted on frozen seas of blood superfused with blood fresh flowing. The same ferocious animal leaves the impression of its broad and heavy foot on the snow of the Arctic Circle and of the Caucasus. And is this indeed all that Europe had brought forth, after such long and painful throes? Has she endured her Marats, her Robespierres, her Buonapartes, for this? God inflicted on the latter of these wretches his two greatest curses; uncontrolled power and perverted intellect; and they were twisted together to make a scourge for a nation which revelled in every crime, but above all in cruelty. It was insufficient. She is now undergoing from a weaker hand a more ignominious punishment, pursued by the derision of Europe. To save her honour, she pretended to admire the courage that decimated her children: to save her honour, she now pretends to admire the wisdom that imprisons them. Cunning is not wisdom; prevarication is not policy; and (novel as the notion is, it is equally true) armies are not strength: Acre and Waterloo show it, and the flames of the Kremlin and the solitudes of Fontainebleau. One honest man, one wise man, one peaceful man, commands a hundred millions, without a baton and without a charger. He wants no fortress to protect him: he stands higher than any citadel can raise him, brightly conspicuous to the most distant nations, God's servant by election, God's image by beneficence.

Landor

---

[1] 'Slaves, gather herbs, scatter incense' (Horace, Odes I, xix, 14).

In Memory of Walter Savage Landor

Back to the flower-town, side by side,
  The bright months bring,
New-born, the bridegroom and the bride,
  Freedom and spring.

The sweet land laughs from sea to sea,
  Filled full of sun;
All things come back to her, being free;
  All things but one.

In many a tender wheaten plot
  Flowers that were dead
Live, and old suns revive; but not
  That holier head.

By this white wandering waste of sea,
  Far north, I hear
One face shall never turn to me
  As once this year:

Shall never smile and turn and rest
  On mine as there,
Nor one most sacred hand be prest
  Upon my hair.

I came as one whose thoughts half linger,
  Half run before;
The youngest to the oldest singer
  That England bore.

I found him whom I shall not find
  Till all grief end,
In holiest age our mightiest mind,
  Father and friend.

But thou, if anything endure,
  If hope there be,
O spirit that man's life left pure,
  Man's death set free.

Not with disdain of days that were
     Look earthward now;
Let dreams revive the reverend hair,
     The imperial brow;

Come back in sleep, for in the life
     Where thou art not
We find none like thee. Time and strife
     And the world's lot

Move thee no more; but love at least
     And reverent heart
May move thee, royal and released,
     Soul, as thou art.

And thou, his Florence, to thy trust
     Receive and keep,
Keep safe his dedicated dust,
     His sacred sleep.

So shall thy lovers, come from far,
     Mix with thy name
As morning-star with evening-star
     His faultless fame.

                                        Swinburne

                    At the grave of Henry James

Startling the awkward footsteps of my apprehension,
     The flushed assault of your recognition is
     The donnée of this doubtful hour:
O stern proconsul of intractable provinces,
O poet of the difficult, dear addicted artist,
     Assent to my soil and flower.

                                        Auden[1]

[1] Auden later removed this admirable stanza from the poem. It is usually a mistake for elderly authors to mess about with their earlier works.

Midnight, June 30, 1879

[On the death of his brother Charles]

Midnight — in no midsummer tune
   The breakers lash the shores:
The cuckoo of a joyless June
   Is calling out of doors:

And thou hast vanish'd from thine own
   To that which looks like rest,
True brother, only to be known
   By those who love thee best.

Midnight — and joyless June gone by,
   And from the deluged park
The cuckoo of a worse July
   Is calling thro' the dark:

But thou art silent underground,
   And o'er thee streams the rain,
True poet, surely to be found
   When Truth is found again.

And now to these unsummer'd skies
   The summer bird is still,
Far off a phantom cuckoo cries
   From out a phantom hill;

And thro' this midnight breaks the sun
   Of sixty years away,
The light of days when life begun,
   The days that seem to-day,

When all my griefs were shared with thee,
   And all my hopes were thine —
As all thou wert was one with me,
   May all thou art be mine!

Tennyson

George Meredith
1828-1909

Forty years back, when much had place
That since has perished out of mind,
I heard that voice and saw that face.

He spoke as one afoot will wind
A morning horn ere men awake;
His note was trenchant, turning kind.

He was of those whose wit can shake
And riddle to the very core
The counterfeits that Time will break . . .

Of late, when we two met once more,
The luminous countenance and rare
Shone just as forty years before.

So that, when now all tongues declare
His shape unseen by his green hill,
I scarce believe he sits not there.

No matter. Further and further still
Through the world's vaporous vitiate air
His words wing on — as live words will.

May 1909   *Hardy*

Grandeur of Ghosts

When I have heard small talk about great men
I climb to bed; light my two candles; then
Consider what was said; and put aside
What Such-a-one remarked and Someone-else replied.

They have spoken lightly of my deathless friends,
(Lamps for my gloom, hands guiding where I stumble,)
Quoting, for shallow conversational ends,
What Shelley shrilled, what Blake once wildly muttered . . .

How can they use such names and be not humble?
I have sat silent; angry at what they uttered.
The dead bequeathed them life; the dead have said
What these can only memorize and mumble.

Sassoon

Bald heads forgetful of their sins,
Old, learned, respectable bald heads
Edit and annotate the lines
That young men, tossing on their beds,
Rhymed out in love's despair
To flatter beauty's ignorant ear.

They'll cough in the ink to the world's end;
Wear out the carpet with their shoes
Earning respect; have no strange friend;
If they have sinned, nobody knows.
Lord, what would they say
Should their Catullus walk that way?

Yeats

Felix Randal

Felix Randal the farrier, O he is dead then? my duty all ended,
Who have watched his mould of man, big-boned and hardy-handsome
Pining, pining, till time when reason rambled in it and some
Fatal four disorders, fleshed there, all contended?

Sickness broke him. Impatient he cursed at first, but mended
Being anointed and all; though a heavenlier heart began some
Months earlier, since I had sweet reprieve and ransom
Tendered to him. Ah well, God rest him all road ever he offended!

This seeing the sick endears them to us, us too it endears.
My tongue had taught thee comfort, touch had quenched thy tears,
Thy tears that touched my heart, child, Felix, poor Felix Randal;

How far from then forethought of, all thy more boisterous years,
When thou at the random grim forge, powerful amidst peers,
Didst fettle for the great grey drayhorse his bright and battering sandal!

Hopkins

In Aix, what's remembered of Cézanne?
A house to let (with studio) in a garden.
(Meanwhile, 'help yourself to these ripe figs, profitez . . .
And if it doesn't suit, we, Agence Sextus, will find you
                                    another just as good'.)
The years are sown together with thread of the same story;
Beauty picked in a field, shaped, recreated,
Sold and despatched to distant Municipality —
But in the master's town
Merely an old waiter, crossly,
'Of course I knew him, he was a dull silent fellow,
Dead now.'
And Beauty walked alone here,
Unpraised, unhindered,
Defiant, of single mind,
And took no rest, and has no epitaph.

Nancy Cunard

My Father [Herbert Beerbohm Tree]

I cannot think that you have gone away:
You loved the earth and life lit up your eyes,
And flickered in your soul that would surmise
Death as a song, a poem, or a play.
You were reborn afresh with every day,
And baffled fortune in some new disguise.
Ah! can it perish, when the body dies,
Such youth, such love, such passion to be gay?
We shall not see you come to us and leave
A conqueror — nor catch on fairy wing
Some slender fancy — nor new wonders weave
Upon the loom of your imagining.
The world is wearier, grown dark to grieve
Her child that was a pilgrim and a king.

Iris Tree

Glaucus

The various voices are his poem now.

Under the currents, under the shifting lights
Of midway water, rolls his fleshy wreck:
Its gurnard eye reflects those airy heights
Where once it noted white Arcturus set.

Gull-swift and swerving, the wet spirit freed
Skims the huge breakers. Watching at the prow
Of any southbound vessel, sailor, heed
Never that petrel spirit, cruel as pride.

Let no cliff-haunting woman, no girl claim
Kinship with Glaucus, neither sow
The tide with daffodils, nor call his name
Into the wind, for he is glorified —
And cold Aegean voices speak his fame.

Sidney Keyes

At Night

To W.M.
[Her husband Wilfrid Meynell]

Home, home from the horizon far and clear,
   Hither the soft wings sweep;
Flocks of the memories of the day draw near
   The dovecote doors of sleep.

O, which are they that come through sweetest light
   Of all these homing birds?
Which with the straightest and the swiftest flight?
   Your words to me, your words!

Alice Meynell

Wit and Brevity

Talking is often a torment to me. I need days of silence to recover from the futility of words.

Jung

C'est qu'elles [les femmes] sont toujours et partout avides d'émotion: voyez les plaisirs de l'enterrement en Ecosse.

Stendhal

Remind me to look happier tomorrow.

Ludwig II of Bavaria, in a note to a servant

The greatest clerkes are not the wisest men.

Chaucer

Nothing is more terrible than ignorance with spurs on.

Goethe

Remarkable men find remarkable conveniences.

Henry James

Lawyers perhaps deserve a particular indulgence, because they are permitted, nay obliged, by the ethics of their profession to make the best possible case for their clients. This entails defending causes they believe to be bad with arguments they know to be dishonest. Who can be surprised if they sometimes acquire a chronic indifference to principle, and if this occupational disease continues to afflict them when they enter political life?

Raymond Mortimer

Many were the wit-combats betwixt him [Shakespeare] and Ben Jonson, which two I behold like a Spanish great galleon and an English man of war.

Thomas Fuller

La Bible et l'aristocratie se vengent cruellement sur les gens qui croient leur devoir tout.

Stendhal

Whatever a man prays for, he prays for a miracle. Every prayer reduces to this: 'Great God, grant that twice two be not four'.

Turgenev

[111]

[The Webbs' letters] lacked the linguistic vivacity which makes tolerable Shaw's massive boringness.

Robert Skidelsky

'You see, when one's young one doesn't feel part of it yet, the human condition; one does things because they are not for good; everything is a rehearsal. To be repeated ad lib, to be put right when the curtain goes up in earnest. One day you know that the curtain was up all the time. That *was* the performance.'

Sybille Bedford

'A second chance — *that's* the delusion. There never was to be but one. We work in the dark — we do what we can — we give what we have. Our doubt is our passion and our passion is our task. The rest is the madness of art.'

Henry James

'If it be now, 'tis not to come; if it be not to come, it will be now; if it be not now, yet it will come: the readiness is all.'

Shakespeare

It is a fact that it takes experience before one can realise what is a catastrophe and what is not. Children have little faculty of distinguishing between disaster and the ordinary course of their lives.

Richard Hughes

Liberty without obedience is confusion; obedience without liberty is slavery.

William Penn

[112]

To write prose, one must have something to say; but he who has nothing to say can still make verses and rhymes, where one word suggests the other, and at last something comes out which in fact is nothing but looks as if it were something.

Goethe

Victor Hugo était un fou qui se croyait Victor Hugo.

Cocteau

The immediate past, the time that one almost belongs to — almost but not quite — is peculiarly tantalising.

Max Beerbohm

Impossible venir, mensonge suit. Guermantes.

Proust

We drank a few cups of coffee, and then drove to the museum [at Jena]. We saw the anatomical cabinet; various skeletons of animals, modern and primeval; as well as skeletons of men of former ages, on which Goethe remarked that their teeth showed them to have been a very moral race.

Eckermann

One evil in old age is that as your time has come you think every little illness is the beginning of the end. When a man expects to be arrested, every knock at the door is an alarm.

Sydney Smith

[113]

Envoi

Que Dieu daigne vous donner à tous
Mes bons amis
Tout ce qu'il faut de patience
Pour supporter la vie,
D'amour et de bienveillance
Pour la rendre douce et utile,
Et de gaieté
Pour s'en moquer.

Charles Nodier

Acknowledgments

For generous permission to quote copyright material I am extremely grateful to Jane Bailey, Vernon Bartlett, Sybille Bedford, Claire Blunden, Jonathan Cape (for William Plomer), Charles Causley and David Higham Associates, Michael Chapman, Dorothy Collins and A. P. Watt (for G. K. Chesterton), Harry Conway, Christopher Cornford, Jacob Dallyn (for Viola Meynell), Jill Day-Lewis, Phoebe Hesketh and the Enitharmon Press, Paul Hyslop (for Raymond Mortimer), Alison Lowbury and Secker & Warburg (for Andrew Young), Roger Morgan, Nancy Morse (for L. E. Jones), the National Trust and Macmillan (for Kipling), Robert Nye and the New Carcanet Press, A. D. Peters (for Belloc and Beachcomber), Irène de Sola Pinto, Mrs Eva Reichmann (for Max Beerbohm), Routledge & Kegan Paul (for Sydney Keyes), Robert Skidelsky, Martyn Skinner, the Society of Authors (on behalf of the Bernard Shaw estate), Jon Stallworthy and the Oxford University Press, Dame Rebecca West and Virago Press, M. B. Yeats, Anne Yeats, and A. P. Watt.

R. H-D.

Index of Authors

A. E. (George Russell) 81
Arnold, Matthew 95
Auden, W. H. 104

Bailey, John 68, 93
Bartlett, Vernon 94
Baudelaire 2
Beachcomber (J. B. Morton) 30
Bedford, Sybille 112
Beerbohm, Max 9, 13, 27, 113
Belloc, H. 21, 65
Binyon, Laurence 100
Birrell, Augustine 3
Bismarck 4
Blake, William 82, 98
Blunden, Edmund 87
Boswell 49
Brooke, Rupert 65
Browne, Sir Thomas 18
Burney, Fanny 92
Butler, Samuel 3
Byron 23, 96

Carew, William 56
Carlyle, Thomas 2, 4, 5, 21, 35, 50, 51, 52, 92, 97
Causley, Charles 89
Cecil, Lord David 1
Chapman, R. W. 93
Chaucer 110
Chesterton, G. K. 1, 29
Churchill, Winston 9, 48
Cocteau, Jean, 4, 113
Coleridge, Mary 63, 88
Coleridge, S. T. 96
Colman, George 52
Conrad, Joseph 24
Conway, Harry 88
Cornford, Frances 77
Cowley, Abraham 72
Cowper, William 93
Cunard, Nancy 108

Day, Clarence 93
Day Lewis, C. 66
Dickens 8, 73
Dickinson, Emily 21, 22, 58, 60, 64, 82, 83
Donne 34
Dyer, Edward 83

Eckermann, J. P. 113

Flaubert 1, 24, 62
Flecker, J. E. 45
France, Anatole 69
Fuller, Thomas 111

Gibbon 2, 7
Goethe 6, 94, 110, 113
Goldsmith, Oliver 52

Hardy, Thomas 36, 43, 59, 62, 69, 87, 99, 106
Hazlitt 81
Heredia 58
Hesketh, Phoebe 22
Holmes, Mr Justice 25, 26, 28, 36
Hopkins, G. M. 100, 107
Hughes, Richard 112
Hugo, Victor 1, 69

James, Henry 3, 4, 7, 16, 73, 75, 111, 112
Johnson, Samuel 23, 49, 50
Jones, L. E. 80
Jonson, Ben 2, 57, 82
Joubert, Joseph 81
Jung 110

Keyes, Sidney 109
Kingsley, Charles 41
Kipling iii, 71

[116]